The Creative School

This book is about a unique school. It is a school that, despite the increasing pressure put upon it by changes in the curriculum and the organisation of education, has managed to maintain the creative values that have won it international and government recognition.

Written for teachers and headteachers who want to encourage creativity in their schools and classrooms, the book describes:

* the school's culture of holism
* its use and appreciation of its grounds and environment for learning
* its innovative approaches to curriculum organisation
* its appropriation of national initiatives such as the literacy and numeracy hours
* its creative teaching and learning through the eyes of observers, teachers, children and parents.

The success of Coombes School shows that it is possible to combine externally imposed prescription with a set of personal beliefs and values – making a real difference to the quality of teaching and learning. This is an inspirational read.

Bob Jeffrey was a primary school teacher for twenty years before joining The Open University, where he is now a Research Fellow. **Peter Woods** was formerly Professor of Education at The Open University. He is currently Research Professor at the University of Plymouth and has written extensively on creative practices in primary schools.

The Creative School

A framework for success, quality and effectiveness

Bob Jeffrey and Peter Woods

 RoutledgeFalmer
Taylor & Francis Group

LONDON AND NEW YORK

First published 2003 by RoutledgeFalmer
2 Park Square, Milton Park, Abingdon, Oxon OX14 4RN

Simultaneously published in the USA and Canada
by RoutledgeFalmer
270 Madison Avenue, New York, NY 10016

Reprinted 2004 (twice)

RoutledgeFalmer is an imprint of the Taylor & Francis Group

© 2003 Bob Jeffrey and Peter Woods

Typeset in Sabon by Keystroke, Jacaranda Lodge, Wolverhampton
Printed and bound in Great Britain by TJ International, Padstow, Cornwall

British Library Cataloguing in Publication Data
A catalogue record for this book is available from the British Library

Library of Congress Cataloging in Publication Data
A catalogue record for this book has been requested

ISBN 0-415-28215-2 (pbk)
ISBN 0-415-28214-4 (hbk)

To Sue Humphries,
Headteacher of Coombes 1971–2002
and to
The staff, parents, and pupils, past and present, and
to the numerous friends of this school.

Contents

Illustrations

Plates

Figures

Acknowledgements

We have drawn on previously published articles. We are grateful to the editors and publishers for permission to use them here. They are: S. Rowe and S. Humphries (2001) 'Creating a Climate for Learning', in A. Craft, B. Jeffrey and M. Leibling (eds) *Creativity in Education* (London: Continuum); P. Woods, 'The Creative Use and Defence of Space: Appropriation through the Environment', in P. Woods (1995) *Creative Teachers in Primary Schools* (Buckingham: Open University Press); and P. Woods (1999) 'Talking about Coombes: Features of a learning community' in J. Retallick, B. Cocklin and K. Coombe (eds) *Learning Communities in Education*, (London: Routledge).

We are also grateful to Sue Humphries and Sue Rowe at Coombes School for advice and comments during the writing of the book. We also wish to acknowledge the academic support given by Anna Craft and Geoff Troman.

Introduction

This is a book about one particular school, a highly successful one judged by a number of criteria, with a national and international reputation. Its publication will coincide with the retirement of its first long-serving headteacher, and in some ways might be seen as a celebration of her life and work, which has been devoted to the advancement of the school. But the book is more than this, offering to other schools at all levels examples of how creative teachers with their own strong beliefs and values can not only come to terms with a heavily prescriptive programme governed by contrary principles, but to some extent at least incorporate it within their own design.

In recent years, child-centredness, 'Plowdenism', 'progressivism', group teaching, creativity, even the notion of 'relevance' (Woodhead, 1995) have taken a hammering in the government's drive for their limited version of raised standards of education. Teachers have struggled with the degree of prescription and constant overload. Coping is an issue in itself, teachers' creativity being diverted into how to manage. For those who go along with the managerialist, market-orientated, performativist cast of the reforms, there is no problem. But what are those who believe in Montessori, Froebel, Dewey, Vygotsky, Bruner and others to do? Coombes provides one notable approach to a solution, one that salvages the best features of the reforms and embraces them within their own discourse.

Among the lessons to be learned here, we would argue, is the need for teachers to have a strong political consciousness. Education and politics cannot be separated in the current climate, though government reforms are often presented as educational 'common sense' (Woods and Wenham, 1995) – part of the rhetoric or 'spin' to win popular support for them. Teachers need to understand the guiding principles behind them, and how their own compare. From this kind of testing comes a greater explicitness and firmness about their beliefs, followed by a plan of action to secure their implementation. Coombes' teachers were as dismayed as any others by the changes of the late 1980s and early 90s. But they have worked their way through them to, in the early years of the twenty-first century, a position of some personal strength.

Other prominent features of the Coombes approach include the highly imaginative and intensive use of the school grounds, and the way it is incorporated in the curriculum and enhances all aspects of teaching. The development has been over twenty years in the making, and is ongoing. Not all schools will be able to emulate Coombes in this respect. As a rural school it has certain advantages, though it does not have a large amount of space. But it is the mindset that is important, the realisation that all the space that the school occupies is of potential education significance. Even hard tarmac, as Coombes shows with its modification of the playground, can have a number of uses. Where there are other, more natural features available, the ideas given here might provide some inspiration.

This notion of educational space and area runs far beyond the school's grounds. Coombes is a community school in the true sense of the concept, both serving and being served by the whole of the community. There is tremendous resource and goodwill available beyond the school gates, and the staff are constantly alert for how it can be employed in providing uncommon interest, rousing enthusiasm, demonstrating skills, advancing achievement, stimulating thought. Teachers' own education and self-renewal benefits from this activity. All are teachers and all are learners in the Coombes environment. Where a specialist input is wanted and is unavailable within the community, they will go beyond. The school year is punctuated by a number of exciting events. Life at Coombes is never dull.

These teachers have to 'deliver' the National Curriculum, and the literacy and numeracy programmes, just as other schools. How do they do it? At the centre of this endeavour is an imaginative modification of the curriculum which evades its domination by the prescriptive programmes. Like everything else at Coombes, this is an ongoing project, discussed every week. Nothing is allowed to stagnate. Within this organisation the school both meets the demands made on it and accomplishes a great deal of its own projects.

Curriculum organisation at Coombes might seem complicated, but once grasped, one can appreciate the interconnected levels of learning that are involved.

Teaching itself is creative, never formulaic. The aim is 'creative learning', with children coming to own their own knowledge and skills, being enthused and changed by the process, and having some control of the learning process, but under teacher guidance. Personal involvement and exciting events not only stimulate children, but give them something to remember in later life. Learning is very much for life at Coombes. It is a new kind of child-centredness, one, we feel, that is better adapted than the Plowdenism of the 1960s and 70s to the needs of the twenty-first century. Throughout the book, we give examples of Coombes' teaching, most of which, we believe, are available to all primary schools.

In the various researches that we have undertaken in primary schools over the last twenty years, we have found the vast majority of teachers to be dedicated to the basic principles of child-centredness. Many have been frustrated and inhibited. Levels of stress have risen throughout the profession and retention levels among new and experienced teachers fallen (Troman and Woods, 2001). But there are positive ways ahead. Coombes offers one outstanding example.

Methodology

We have been connected with Coombes since 1990, collaborating with teachers in writing articles, book chapters, conference papers and producing Open University films and course material. Between 1999 and 2001, we conducted a sustained ethnographic project aimed at understanding teaching and learning at the school in greater depth. To this end, Bob Jeffrey attended the school for three days each half term over a period of two years. During this period, the school staffing consisted of six full-time teachers and at least five part-time teachers. All the full-time teachers and three of the part-time teachers took part in the research (Figure 1).

One significant fact concerning the Coombes teachers is how often first encounters with the school result in a determination to stay at the school. Final-year teaching-practice students such as Ray and Jo became committed to getting a job there, so much so that Jo took a part-time job in the hope that a full-time one would come later. Parents sometimes stayed on. Sue Rowe, for example, worked as secretary before deciding to train as a teacher. She has now been

Teacher	Age	Original school connection	Years as a teacher	Specialism
Sue Humphries headteacher	50+	Opened Coombes	31	Religious education + environment
Sue Rowe deputy head	40–50	Parent	17	Science + design technology
Judy	40–50	Parent	10	Art + history
Carol	40–50	From college	30	Language + ICT
Carole	30–40	From college	7	Language + geography + drama
Jo	20–30	From college	3	
Jude	30–40	Parent	20	Maths + SENCO
Gill part time	30–40	From college	25	Music + INSET
Jenny part time	50+	Parent	25	Physical education
Ray part time	20–30	From college	11	
Anne part time	30–40	Parent	4	
Ann	30–40	From college	10	Nursery Coordinator

Figure 1 Coombes teaching staff, 2001

appointed to the headship following Sue Humphries' retirement in December 2002.

Data collection was through qualitative methods, consisting chiefly of interviews with teachers, support workers, parents, children and visitors. The earlier research, in the first part of the 1990s, focused on teacher creativity and how the school adjusted to the government's reforms. We were more concerned in the later research period with the children's experience of creative teaching, focusing on their perspectives, recorded through extensive field notes. We collected relevant documentation such as newsletters, governors' and inspectors' reports, timetables, school-policy statements and national test results. We used photographs extensively as data and as stimulants for exploring children's perspectives. At one stage, children were given cameras to select their own observations for discussion. By comparing the various different kinds of data, both within and across cases, we were able to identify prominent issues and themes connected to our major subject of creative teaching and learning and the effects this has on the various participants.

An additional feature of the research was the extent of collaboration sought with the teachers. To this end we worked with them on the research design, identifying objectives and setting priorities. We reported to staff meetings, circulated memos and papers to staff and invited them to present their perspectives at conferences we organised. This was for a number of reasons, first outlined in our more general research into creative teaching and the National Curriculum (Woods and Jeffrey, 1996). Firstly, it seemed ethically appropriate. We worked closely with these teachers for long periods in their schools and we viewed them as highly skilled and accomplished professionals. Consequently, we believed that they had a vital interest in the outcomes of the research that was based on their work. Secondly, they represented a resource, with particular knowledge, skills and insight, that could be put into the research that was different from that of us, the researchers, but just as valuable in its own way. Thirdly, we see a major purpose of our research as feeding back into schools and teaching, and we feel this needs to be carried out through teachers if it is to have any effect. Our teachers are sharing their views and experiences not only with us, but with their fellow professionals elsewhere, for them to discuss and incorporate into their own perspectives and cultures (Fullan and Hargreaves, 1992). Fourthly, like critical theorists (Gitlin, 1990; Smythe, 1991; Kincheloe, 1993), we are opposed to elitist, hierarchical forms of research which exploit 'subjects' for academics' own benefit. We are conscious of what Fine (1994) describes as 'othering' – seeing teachers as completely separate and different from us, the researchers. A fifth, and related, point, is that we were only too conscious that we were two males researching an area entirely staffed by women. One way in which we could seek to compensate for this was to co-opt the teachers on to the research. Another was to ensure that the point was a regular item on the agendas of our research meetings, together with reflection on possible influences on the research.

Structure of the book

In Chapter 1, we describe the ethos of the school, which is immediately apparent as one approaches its boundaries. Children and adults will often be seen working in the grounds of the school, and as one enters the school a dynamism of activity, a welcoming gesture and immediate involvement is experienced. This open and engaging ethos is exemplified by the extensive involvement of members of the community and worldwide guests who are to be seen, on most days, contributing to the school's curriculum and permeating the school's teaching and learning practices. The distinctiveness of Coombes is explained in terms of its approach to policy, curriculum and pedagogy.

In Chapter 2, we discuss the creative development of the school grounds, which has been a major feature of Coombes' history. In more ways than one, it contextualises the school and its activities. Apart from ministering to the teachers' strong interest in environmental education, the grounds provide an enormously valuable resource for all curriculum areas. We examine the nature of this development and the principles behind it. The number and variety of plants, trees, shrubs, flowers, ponds, paths and other constructions in such a limited space is amazing, and all designed for teaching in a systematic way. The development has been ongoing since the school opened and is still unfinished – it is a perennial project, a growing thing and a source of delight and inspiration for teachers and children alike. The aim is to involve the children in the real world with hands-on activities to bring into play all their senses, to liberate their thoughts and feelings, and to stimulate their minds. In keeping with Coombes' holistic approach, its use of the grounds is totally integrated within the curriculum. The school thus provides one example of how an overfull, compartmentalised National Curriculum (Campbell *et al.*, 1991) can be brought together into a coherent whole.

The introduction of the National Curriculum in 1989 followed quickly by national assessment programmes and national (Ofsted) and local inspections, faced Coombes with a challenge to its distinctive approach to teaching and learning. Instead of just rejecting or accepting the reforms, Coombes sought ways of meeting the prescribed governmental demands while sustaining its own values in its educational practices, even though it seemed to borrow from conflicting philosophies. We consider in Chapter 3 the micro-political processes involved in their 'appropriation' of the reforms – ways in which the school sought to make the reforms work in its, Coombes', way. The process of appropriation involves recognition of the political aspects of the reforms and the learning theories behind them. It also entails, by comparison, sharper definition of one's views and principles, and, with that, a stiffening personal and corporate resolve. It was from a position of some mental and moral strength, therefore, that Coombes' teachers 'engaged' with the National Curriculum. They sought to teach it creatively, adventurously, interestingly, and in ways that would lead children to integrate personal knowledge. Finally, Coombes has built up a number of alliances – with, for example, school governors, parents, inspectors – which serve both to reinforce its approach to the prescribed curriculum and assessment, and to provide a strong local political base.

In Chapter 4, we show how the school responded radically by reorganising its whole curriculum structure in an innovative manner whilst continuing to maintain the interest it had in being 'child considerate'. It is rather a complicated arrangement, sustained by everyday discussion about the contingencies of the moment. There are class groups with their own class teacher for registration and other activities; age cohorts for the core curriculum subjects of literacy and numeracy, where they go to other teachers; and mixed age groups for other curriculum subjects. A significant proportion of time is set aside for considered needs of the moment. In addition there are special events, termly themes and subject days. The aim is to maximise the resources of the school, to provide variety and novel experiences for the children, to ensure that the prescribed demands of the National Curriculum are met but in an interesting, exciting and meaningful way. The aim is also to maintain creative activities such as art and music and to provide a many-sided and multi-levelled education but in an integrated way. One of the ways this is done is through what we term 'network learning' involving net-like structures of knowledge and multiple perspectives apprehended through all the senses.

The main test of success of any school is in the effect it has on pupils' learning. Creative teaching needs to lead to creative learning. In Chapter 5 we provide details of the impact of Coombes' teaching on the children, what learning means to the children, and what part the children themselves play in the development of knowledge and pedagogy. The essence of teaching and learning at Coombes lies in its authenticity, in the provision of real-world and real-life experiences. Real learning and children's personal knowledge are encouraged through hands-on, active engagements, through role play, and through generating positive feelings about learning. Learning is exciting, fun, inspiring, rewarding and motivating. Through providing a range of opportunities for children along these lines, Coombes has developed an 'adventure culture' of new experiences for the discovery of new knowledge, skills, talents, abilities and interests. Children are encouraged to be creative, to play with ideas, to take risks and to use their imaginations. Through doing so, children transform knowledge into meaning and structure that has relevance within their own perspectives. They make knowledge their own. But it is knowledge that has social and communal currency, fostered through the equally strong collaborative culture of learning, not only among and between teachers and children, but involving all members of the community. These are the features of a reconstructed progressivism, a child-considered, rather than child-centred, education. Coombes has performed well on official tests and inspections. The kind of qualitative evaluations contained in this chapter demonstrate their broader and deeper accomplishment.

In Chapter 6, we consider some of the factors that make Coombes a successful school. The most prominent feature here is its strongly developed and maintained state as a learning community. As such, it constitutes one possible model for future primary schooling. At its heart is a visionary leader, the long-serving head of Coombes, who had a 'plan' from the very beginning, one that was to grow and grow until it provided its own momentum. Sue also has uncommon abilities, especially in inspiring others and in getting things done, however unusual or impossible they might seem. A strong team has supported her, teachers in her own image, also long-serving and equally dedicated to the values and beliefs they all share. The team operates through democratic participation within a culture of collaboration, which has proved a useful mode for developing, releasing and supporting the creativity of all its members. Governors, parents and members of the community are embraced within a larger team, all working in and for the same project, all contributing to, and benefiting from, the Coombes spirit. It is a community where all are teachers and learners, and they all teach and learn a wide range of skills and knowledge within an integrated framework. The whole community is tapped for what it can contribute towards the Coombes project, the school, in turn, giving back a sense of reward, fellowship and ownership to the community. Finally, no school can survive these days on educational principles alone. The successful school requires a keen political consciousness, and, especially where its principles are at some variance with those of a centralising government, something of a local power base.

Chapter 1

The Coombes ethos

Visitors to Coombes County Infant and Nursery School at Arborfield, near Reading, encounter a very distinctive atmosphere. It is to do with the activities that are taking place, some of them quite unusual; with the large numbers of involved adults; with the disposition of children and adults, the relationships among them and how they react together; with contexts, décor, illustrations, teaching aids; and with how you are greeted and welcomed. As you go through the day, moving from one intriguing event or situation to another, the charismatic climate seems to be 'coming out of the walls' (parent). An ethos is something that is felt rather than thought. The most prominent features of this ethos, therefore, carry a strong emotional theme. They are dynamism, appreciation, captivation and care.

A dynamic ethos

There is a continuous throb of movement and a quiet hum of activity. It is a corporeal ethos as children stretch, jump, slide, tiptoe, step cautiously, hold hands, fiddle with each other's hair and lift and swing each other round. Smiles, welcomes and laughter pervade the school. Young children are energetic people, forever moving their bodies and minds across the space they inhabit, experiencing the delights of physical expression and the excitement of encountering and engaging with new phenomena. The school understands young children as active agents who experiment with their bodies, emotions and intellects. Teachers acknowledge the enormous capacity of young children to take in an extensive variety of experiences in any one day. 'You can walk in and find one group of children with magnets all over the floor, another doing things with keys, others working with stinging nettles, or weaving and harvesting, or counting sunflower seeds' (parent).

When Sue Rowe (deputy head) first visited the school as a prospective parent,

> it was the playground developments that immediately arrested the eye, and made one think, 'What's happening here?' That rich quality of environment outside the school made you want to go indoors and see what was happening. That day was actually Hallowe'en, and everyone was dressed up, there were children diving their heads in and apple-bobbing, and teachers with green faces and wild hair, and the place was humming, really humming. And it's like that most days, most weeks. There's a dynamic centre to the week.

An appreciative ethos

Coombes's ethos is also 'appreciative'. The ecological environment, social interactions, spiritual narratives, the skills and crafts of the community, cycles of life and annual cultural celebrations are all appreciated for their uniqueness and their signification. Everyone, including parents, enjoy the 'grand' events that permeate most weeks of the year and the policy of a 'hands-on' approach ensures that children's curiosity is stimulated and satisfied. Pleasure is gained from many adventures: seeing a 'Coombeshenge' rise before their eyes in the grounds; helping to cut down the Christmas tree, planting daffodils, potatoes, sunflowers; 'beating the bounds' of the school site with long sticks and returning to one of the many annual events, such as the Epiphany march around the grounds in January. Appreciation involves understanding, awareness, discernment and insight as each new engagement not only reveals features and qualities of itself but joins with all the other engaging experiences to comprehend the breadth of the world and the delights of learning.

Every week, people visit the school to talk about their lives, perform their skills and reproduce their crafts – Irish dancers, Scottish bagpipe performers, harpists, artists, stone masons, a military band, a bell-ringing group, a vet ministering to the sheep, a member of the Cromwell society on a horse, a crew in an army helicopter, a juggler on a one-wheel bike, a specialist in children's playground songs and rhymes from America, a Muslim woman talking about her faith and culture. There are also environmental maintenance events such as sheep-shearing, hedge-building, and willow-arch-weaving. These talks, demonstrations or performances engage the children's interest and take them on something akin to a 'Grand Tour' of the world outside the school:

> In the sea-shanty experience instructors talked above the children and alongside them as they tapped their feet, wiggled their hips, practised dance steps, shook arms, jumped up and down, stretched legs, twisted and turned and swung their arms. They experimented by running too far and exaggerating their arm movements while marching. In a smaller dance group some had thumbs in their mouths as they concentrated on dance instructions and their eyes scrutinised the performers as they anticipated participation. As the dance movements were explained they whispered quietly and experimented with their arms and feet. They focused intently on the detail of the playing instruments when invited to ask questions.
>
> (Field note)

The dancing to and singing of sea shanties lasted for forty minutes in each classroom and at the end of the day all the school gathered together in the hall to perform and exhibit their new skills and knowledge. Parents collecting their children were exhorted to join in this activity.

New themes, or new ways of approaching the same themes are deliberate policy. Teachers believe in 'first-class experiences for adults and children, so that they can resonate with those experiences and be energised next day'. A concert, for example, provided 'valuable reflective time, a chance to reorganise their thinking, to be refreshed, and up-and-running the next day'. It might take you away from a task, but 'you get back to it with renewed vigour'. Sue Humphries (headteacher) 'believed passionately in the ability of certain experiences to regenerate everyone', 'reflective nuggets' she called them, which were 'even more important now than formerly because of the mechanistic approaches induced by current developments'.

Community-engaging events are a central feature of the regular curriculum cycle – Valentine's Day, saints' days, religious festivals and national events including Bastille Day. Lifelong learning days are held annually where extended families join in the curriculum as well as creating it. A technology week is held where children bring in 'carriers' and employ them to transport the ripe pumpkins from the grounds for Hallowe'en, and planting and harvesting are eagerly anticipated as part of the school's cycle of events.

These events constitute an everyday community knowledge, a 'common-sense' knowledge (Bernstein, 1971) of the pupils, their families and peer groups:

> It's a sense of being engaged and intrigued by work that goes on around them. It's coming into them from the community, via a national world, and via a National Curriculum. It is by encouraging other nationals, by encouraging people with a mark for talent, whether it's sowing, knitting, or writing poetry. They are being connected to much wider artistic, work and spiritual concerns. In this way they are learning more than the National Curriculum, which I hope we are doing well, but these others are equally important, as is nursing the side of the child that is going to be empathetic, imaginative and tolerant.
>
> (Sue Humphries)

A captivating ethos

Coombes embraces pupils, parents and teachers alike. Jenny has been at the school for twenty-six years:

> I brought my eldest daughter, Jo, as a rising five to the Coombes, and came in as a helping mum, the way we encourage all mums to come in and help, and I've been here ever since.

Ray was a student at the school. On the first day she thought it was

> wonderful. The children just seemed really happy, the staff were really, really welcoming, and I could see children using the grounds in such a creative way, I just knew that I wanted to come back, so as soon as there was a place I got back in. I've loved it.

Sue Rowe was similarly captivated:

> I think it was my experience here as a mother, coming in to help, and seeing a style of education that I didn't realise existed anywhere, and becoming increasingly involved.

Navnite (parent) had found children in other schools withdrawn and reserved, but here,

> it was very natural, it had a certain sort of ambience about it. There's nothing fabricated or set up, to me it's just another home away from home because there is so much emphasis on loving, caring and sharing. It's just like a whole big family, it's not like individual children, it's everyone together.

The magnetism of the school also works for the shy child. Dee's daughter was 'painfully shy' and found it 'very difficult to mix with people'. Sue Humphries suggested they spend a day with her prospective class:

> I stayed for a bit, then I realised that I could sneak off, she was completely absorbed in what was going on. I came back a little later and she didn't even notice I was there. I decided there and then it was completely what I was looking for. Within a week of her starting here they were making pumpkin soup, then they were burning down houses and eating baked potatoes, then they were moving into the Christmas stuff and I was just like 'Wow! What's this about'?

Martin found

> the buzz, this unknown quantity that you just cannot put your finger on. It just exudes from the walls of the building. There's a magic formula.

The whole community has been captivated by Coombes. Sue Humphries spoke of the 'tremendous support' they received from parents. 'If you organise it, you make the whole community part of the work'. An illustration of Sue's opportunism was given during the sheep-washing. Limara said, 'My mummy washes her own hair, and she used to be a hairdresser'. 'Aha!' said Sue, 'I have an idea. If we asked her to come in, would she give us a demonstration? I'll volunteer to have my hair done!' Thus are ideas generated to sustain the flow of interaction between school and community, and between school work and everyday life. There were frequent 'displays of community affection which hasn't dwindled a bit', and a 'very impressive underground network which reaches out to people miles away and pulls them in to serve the school's traditions'.

Sue spoke of 'days of excitement, when it works for all of you – pupils, teachers, parents – as a kind of yeast'. There was an open door for parents to enter the school to observe or to assist. The school was a 'laboratory for anyone who steps over the door. If people feel that they want to do something, the more people develop a sense of ownership – an ownership action plan – we're all going to be better off for it' (Sue Humphries). This is another aspect of the holism that pervades the underlying philosophy, involving all who have links with the school in whatever role. On special-event days (see Chapter 4), when extra adult help was required, they turned out in force. But they were free to use and enjoy the grounds themselves. Sue has fond ideas of an 'open school' for use by the community in the evening, perhaps as a place for youngsters to use.

The sense of an 'extended family' here is typical of a learning community (see, for example, Cocklin *et al.*, 1996). It runs counter to the kind of school whose function is mainly to separate children from families and to introduce them to wider society (Macbeth, 1994). The latter is a more traditional view of school, with a 'boundary' set up between the school and the outside world, and between teachers and parents. But the Coombes community would not recognise these divisions. They would argue that the interests of society – and of individuals – is better served by combining forces.

However, they also recognise the need to ensure a secure and safe environment for the children. All regular visitors are vetted according to the local education authority's guidelines and new visitors have to sign in and wear badges of identification. In appropriate cases groups of visitors are assigned to school staff for the time they are in the school. The reality of Coombes' open policy is that the extensive number of adults on the school site means that it is highly unusual for any adult to be found alone with children. There is almost always more than one adult with any group of children and the rooms have been designed to be easily viewed by those passing by.

A caring ethos

Audrey (parent) was 'overwhelmed by what a positive experience it obviously was for all the children'. She thought it was a matter of caring and respect:

> The fundamental thing is that children are taught to care for each other and to share everything and so they're taught respect for themselves and respect for other people and respect for the environment.

Carol affirmed, 'There's a very, very strong emphasis on caring'. Martin was impressed with the continuity of learning, stemming from the open policy of the school:

> The school is exceptional in the way they welcome children and parents and anybody that's associated with a particular child into the school. Making them welcome makes them want to be part of the school, makes them want to learn and take in and share everything they learn here. So they come home and they tell us about it, we talk to them about it, and they come back again the following day and explain again what they have learned. It's just a continuation. They don't actually leave school. We're very pleased with all aspects of work, play, and caring and sharing and being part of an extended family. She doesn't feel as if she is coming to school, she's just coming to another part of her family, and when she comes home to us she comes back to the other part of her family. She's got no problem with crossing the boundary of the school gates.

Cath had recently moved to the area. She came to Coombes to look round and found:

> They were so very kind when we came in. I walked into the wrong classroom, and they said, 'Oh Mark, I hope you come into *this* class', and I just thought, 'They're so very friendly'. At his previous school he cried for the whole week! At least when he came here, he cried for one day, and the next day he was quite happy to go to school.

When Theresa phoned up for an appointment she was told, 'You don't need an appointment. Turn up whenever you like, go wherever you like'. She found, 'you can just wander around, but if you ask if you can help they will find something for you. So you get very involved.' Sidone found the same. She had not enjoyed school herself, and 'always felt on edge walking into a school', but 'when I walked in here they're just so friendly. I really value the fact that I can walk in at any time and join in. That means a lot to me'.

Beryl Ellinor (school governor), reflecting on why Coombes was such a special school, concluded

> There's a lot of love in this school, and I think that's what draws me to it particularly. Because we all need love and this school does generate a great deal. It's the dedication of the headteacher and her staff. The parents that are so willing to help, the other members of the community are willing to help, and the well-being and the way that children learn and the way they're so happy, it's – well – it's magic!

Linda (teaching assistant) felt similarly, 'It's a very loving friendly atmosphered school. I love it. As you walk through the front door there's a friendly atmosphere that seems to envelop you.'

The distinctiveness of Coombes

Coombes has over two hundred pupils, from a mixed rural catchment area. Its children (3–7 years old) are nearly all from the white majority ethnic group including approximately 40 per cent of its pupils from the local army garrison and a regular group of traveller children. Both groups are prone to move regularly and consequently the school has a relatively high transient population. Its staff are well established in their posts. Coombes has won national and international acclaim. It is rather an unusual school. It attracts approximately a thousand visitors a year from all over the world and its staff give courses and lectures about the school and its teaching in many countries. It has won a number of awards, notably a prestigious Jerwood Award in 1990. Its longstanding headteacher, Sue Humphries, was awarded an MBE in 1995 for outstanding services to education. Coombes features regularly in the educational press, has been the subject of television programmes, for example, an Open University course (E208, TV21, 'A School for our Times') and has been written about (Woods 1995; Rowe and

Humphries, 2001; Jeffrey, 2001). A reconstruction of part of the garden, which included home-grown sunflowers and garden sounds was exhibited at the Hampton Court flower show in 2002 and televised. It serves regularly as a site for field trips for other schools.

We shall attempt to present the essential features that make it an outstanding school, and to discern what all schools can learn from Coombes' experiences of teaching and learning. These features are in three main areas.

Policy

In 1998 the Secretary of State for Education set up a National Advisory Committee to report and make recommendations on 'the creative and cultural development of young people through formal and informal education'. The resulting report, entitled *All our Futures: Creativity, Culture and Education* (NACCCE, 1999) strongly argued the case for more creativity within education. Coombes offers one case of how this might be achieved within the context of the National Curriculum and national assessment. Coombes' teachers have shown remarkable creativity and energy in incorporating the government's initiatives into the school's organisation while reconstructing their own values. The school could therefore provide a touchstone for the development of a new kind of primary school, one which both reflects the official policy discourse and illustrates how schools can influence, evaluate and reconstruct that discourse.

Pedagogy

Coombes teachers have developed what might be termed a 'reconstructed progressivism'. Much of the debate on teaching has been conducted in terms of polarities or dichotomies: traditional versus progressive; child-centred versus curriculum or teacher-centred; instruction versus discovery; holism versus compartmentalisation; individual versus whole-class teaching; phonics versus good books; managerialism versus professionalism; economic rationalism versus humanism. This debate on the whole does more harm than good, and is responsible for the pendulum swings between traditionalism and progressivism that typify the English educational system. Educational advance, we would argue, depends on a subtle balance between the two, something many primary teachers have tried to attain, with varying success. Again, Coombes' teachers rise above this debate and offer a solution in developing a 'structured child-centredness' (Sugrue, 1998).

Curriculum

Most primary schools adhere to the National Curriculum and the literacy and numeracy programmes. Whatever the merits of these initiatives, there has been criticism from many schools that there have been too many of them and that they have been too directive, thus impeding teachers' own creativity and narrowing the general curriculum, with many valuable subject areas and activities being lost or squeezed. The value of Coombes lies in the creative ways it has appropriated these policies, doing what is required but doing much more besides. Other schools may be very interested to learn exactly how Coombes' teachers have organised their curriculum in order to achieve this.

Chapter 2

Learning through the environment

The creative use of space

Coombes has acquired international recognition for the imaginative development of its school grounds. A *Learning through Landscapes* report (Adams, 1990) records that 'an immense variety of environments have been established, using every available inch of space'. Sue Humphries sums up their policy:

> We see the outside of the school as a wealthy resource, which can be drawn upon, if we are prepared to plan its development. We wanted the outside environment to reflect the same degree of care and imagination that was given to other areas of the school.

In this chapter, we consider the Coombes achievement and the factors behind it. We describe the planning and nature of the grounds, and examine the learning principles behind them. There are two groups of these connected with 'involvement' on the one hand, and 'holism' on the other, with the major theme of 'environmentalism' running through them both. These lead to 'inspiration', and all produce 'creative learning'.

The school grounds – a creative use of space

Coombes opened in 1971 on a small, flat, barren site seeded with rye grass and edged with chain-link boundaries, and depleted through the ravages of builders. Every year since then, the school, under the guidance of Sue Humphries has worked to develop the grounds into an area of beauty in its own right and a rich resource for learning and development. Through the years, teachers and children have worked together in producing 'a living time-line'. The grounds represent the history of the school. The layout at the time of writing is depicted in Figure 2.

The grounds are 'planted for teaching' in a systematic way, since what impressed them most at the beginning was that 'the school should be set in a wood – its kindergarten'. Trees in the grounds represent all the common species of northern Europe. There is a profusion of spring-flowering bulbs, two wild-flower meadows, sunflowers, pumpkins, herbs, fruit bushes, vegetable plots, a rock garden, five ponds, hedges, animal enclosures (for sheep), herbs, an ivy garden (where the spiders live), a minibeast sanctuary, a maze, compost heaps, a ditch, clay pit, earth mounds, nut orchard and many nooks and crannies. All this hosts a world of life, including fungi, algae, mosses, butterflies, moths, birds and a variety of small mammals. A simple inventory, however, cannot do justice to the planning of the site. All-weather pathways with a range of surfaces (concrete, bark chipping, timber planking, gravel chips, etc.) take us round, bringing us close to the various features, through oak, larch, Norway spruce, black poplar, hazel, silver birch, willow, blackthorn and hornbeam. The trail is wooded nearly all the way round, skirting the playground, bringing you near the ponds but keeping 'discrete boundaries' for safety purposes, and close to the animal pens. At points along the path 'time capsules' are buried – biscuit tins containing work from child and adult 'for future historians'.

Sue Humphries explained how she had 'extended' the small area allocated to the school by introducing a system of banking. When the school was first built

> There was no back drive down – we made that ourselves; and the site was totally flat and everything was on straight planes.
>
> The area doesn't alter but by the introduction of a few mounds and troughs you get a bigger area and you get micro-climates. If a stepped bank faces south or north nature's very susceptible to the slightest change such as the wind reaching the plants, or the length of sunlight, amount of light or shadow.

In this way she had created space in the narrow spit of land between the school and the road:

> You've got a *tromp l'œuil* effect. From the spot we stand to the road is no distance, but by filling the middle ground you create

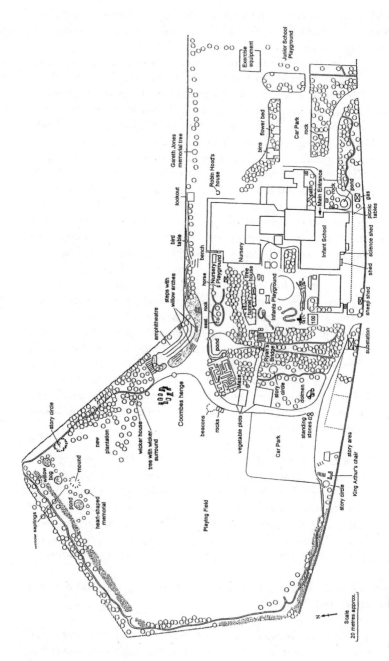

Figure 2 The school grounds

a depth that isn't there at all. It's surprising how the arrangement of forms and a planting scheme create this powerful
illusion.

She has some old photographs with the buildings on the other side
of the road, and 'they surprise you because you realise how close
everything is to you'.

Aconites, snowdrops, crocuses and narcissi flower before the
trees are in leaf. They are set in natural drifts so you can see and
smell them, avoiding the formal ranks of town parks. The aim is
for a 'natural profusion of spring flowers to delight eyes and
hearts'. On one side is 'a shelter-belt so the wind doesn't scour the
playground'. There is even a 'secondary shelter-belt' behind. The
playground was 'not very hospitable' to begin with, and 'the centre
must be kept open because it's tarmac, can't be colonised easily'
and the children need the space to play in all weathers. You can
plant trees around the edges to

> provide constant contact with the plants and the smells and
> the changing forms all the time. The idea is to put children in a
> woodland setting where, around the hard edges of the play-
> ground, trees droop, drop leaves, shed blossom, produce apples.
> Plants in the gardens offer different smells to attract insects,
> birds and humans, and if you want to go on a ladybird safari or
> you want to do snail racing, it's all available to you.

The school site has to be 'managed'. Coppicing and pollarding
are regularly carried out on some of the trees. Coppicing involves
cutting the tree back and induces the 'throwing of a lot of new spurs,
providing very good cover for birds, and better nesting potential'.
Pollarding removes the crown of a tree (preventing it growing too
tall) and it then sends out new branches from the top of the stem.
Willows are treated in this way, the cut branches then providing
nourishing food for the sheep. Sue herself comes out with secateurs
occasionally but to do several things, including 'preventing the horse
chestnuts coming through, and anything that is an alien, such as
laburnum or sumach that come in with the leaf litter'.

The school explains its aims and strategies, and the central
philosophy thus:

> Learning, play and dreaming have a unity, which inspire each
> other. Adults tend to separate the parts, children do not. We

help them stretch their intellectual powers by teaching out-of-doors and organising natural renewable resources in the same careful way as with organising an indoor classroom. Fruit trees bloom and fruit over pathways; maths diagrams cover the tarmac; old logs and low walls provide seating, and there are many places to hide and be silent. It is continually evolving by adding new trees, new playground designs, different play-ground furniture – and by seasonal changes, daylight length, plant growth, and animal and insect activity. The hard spaces are framed by gardens and woodland areas and protected by them. All provide easy hand, eye, ear and nose contact and feed the intellectual, emotional and spiritual elements. Around the playground are boats, walls, logs, stepping-stones, a tunnel, a bird wall, buildings (a castle, a look-out post, a cave, a play table, a house and three tree houses), all designed to excite the imagination and interest, and provide lots of dramatic play.

The playground is marked out with designs for games collected from around the world: Pong Hau Ki, a Schlegel diagram, Nine Man's Morris, Achi, Star, concentric circles, a number snake, a hundred square, a chess board (with pieces made by a parent), a logic track and a compass rose (a guide to the school's position). Whenever the weather permits, the children eat out of doors, under the canopy of the trees. Dinner supervisors bring out the tables and put them on the pathways. Occasionally they set up old carpets under the trees for the children to sit on.

Sue points to how things could have been improved, for example:

> The pinetum should have been extended by another five or six metres, so that there would have been nothing in this area except cone-producing trees. You could have gone from tree to tree, looked at the characteristics and noted the similarities and differences. Again, it would have been better to group silver birch together with the holly so that there was an aesthetic keynote there. You'd have grouped the species of oaks together so that you could move from tree to tree, showing children how they differed.

She hopes others learn from these points. The site is still developing. For example, she pointed to the trees lining the drive, 'Eventually these trees will arch and join up, and give the sensation of an old country lane'.

The usual practice is for school playgrounds to be regular – rectangular or square. Even those playgrounds with some variation in shape tend to follow straight lines. In general, the edges of the playground are difficult to maintain because the grass gets eroded. In the wet weather it is mud, and in the dry weather, dust. Coombes has deregularised its playground shape. The playground edges do not lead directly on to the gardens. The whole playground is surrounded by barriers behind which planting takes place. The idea of the barrier (in most cases, a 60 cm high double-course brick wall indented to provided niches for small-group play and gatherings) is to give accessible seating at any moment during play. Additionally, the children can climb on to the walls to have a different perspective on the playground, or they may choose to lie flat on the top. The barrier serves as a series of ready-made shelves upon which apparatus may be set, or a book display exhibited.

What was once a rectangular play space has been indented. On the north side there are broad steps leading to two tree houses, as well as a tunnel leading to a back pathway, and an access point to the field area. On the west side there is a 'castle' and a terrace area. On the south side there are two large raised beds planted with herbs, fruit trees and slow-growing dwarf conifers. On the east side there is a garden enclosed by a crenellated brick wall. The children do not enter this small garden which is planted with holly, hazel, silver birch and apple trees, but may reach into it for ladybirds, snails, leaves, etc. The crenellations are ornamental and provide seating at different heights, but they also inhibit children from running on the top. The planting which has taken place in the garden areas immediately behind the wall barriers has served to soften the playground edges, to protect the children from the prevailing wind, and to reach out into the playground itself. Many of the trees blossom and shower the children with petals.

Though Coombes is not over-endowed with space, the development of the grounds is an ongoing project, a living thing in itself. Sue and Sue write,

> Over the years, we have undertaken a programme of environmental planting and improvement. Our school grounds, and the diversity of habitats contained within them, are essential components of our work with the children. Each term over the

years has seen at least one major project undertaken, and often the stimulus for the project will have come directly from the children's suggestions or from a perceived curricular need. Sometimes, development work will take place because of a previous addition to our gardens and grounds, which leads us on to the next stage. For instance, we have created a series of all-weather pathways that criss-cross the school grounds; as each section is completed, the site of the next needed pathway becomes more apparent.

Sometimes, the next phase will be the result of a chance comment from a member of staff, a parent or governor, or a visitor to the school. We make progress in our environmental work by remaining open to new ideas, suggestions, or by evaluating what we have been doing and looking to take the work onwards. Comments about needing to do something special for the Millennium led us to the idea of setting up a geology trail throughout the grounds – at least 12 different types of rock from the British Isles set in different ways. To date, and with six months of the year still to go, we now have seven groups of rock ranging from Cornish arranged as a platform seating area, to Purbeck limestone set as 'King Arthur's Chair' on a small artificial hill, to Yorkshire limestone samples set in a formation similar to the central circle of Stonehenge – our very own Coombeshenge. Sometimes, it is the children themselves who come up with the ideas that take us into the next bit of environmental work. Recently they asked for a tree house with a tree growing through the middle, and we are now in the process of building it.

(Rowe and Humphries, 2001, pp. 169–70)

Some pupils have experienced schools as alien, imprisoning places from which they have been glad to escape at the end of the day back into the real, natural world (see, for example, Woods, 1995, ch. 6). Coombes aims to be 'real' and 'natural', offering a resource which many might have assumed would be more 'normally' available beyond the boundaries of institutional life. It also enriches not only the official side of school, but also the informal. Even when used just for playtimes, research among 7-year-olds has shown that playtime and dinner take up 28 per cent of the school day (Tizzard et al., 1988). The quality of interaction might be variable, with bullying and fights prominent (ibid.).

It is also an arena for the transmission of cultural information, especially about gender (Grugeon, 1988, 1993). Further, teachers seem to feel that the quality of children's interaction is declining (Blatchford, 1989). Pressures in the National Curriculum have led to demands that playtimes be reduced (Ashley, 1993). The character of schools has altered in response to the National Curriculum and in particular to the standardised tests by which school performance is measured. Coombes' staff feel that it is now even more essential that the children and staff have immediate access to living, growing things in the school setting. They argue that being able to move around in a soft, natural landscape leads to feelings of well-being and provides a counterbalance to stress and formal demands made on both pupils and staff.

Research by Blatchford *et al.* (1990) showed that children themselves wanted, among other things, more permanent equipment, better game markings, 'green' additions and structural changes – items provided at Coombes. Thus children's informal interaction, as well as their formal education, stands to be enriched by these developments. Coombes sees playtimes as not only worthwhile but essential for learning.

Learning principles

Clearly, the intention of this kind of development is to give children a multi-sensory education. It is also strongly motivated by love of, and concern for, the environment, and the desire to give children a good start to becoming environmentally literate. It speaks to one of the major issues confronting the world today. It is one of the cross-curricular themes in the National Curriculum. But it is not only an issue and a theme. It is also a major resource for learning in general, equivalent to the indoor library, informing the whole of the curriculum and of life. There are three major principles underpinning the teaching approach to the construction and use of the grounds – involvement, holism and inspiration. The first two produce the third.

Involvement

One of the school's handbooks affirms that

> Children will not easily be persuaded by adult talk, by reading books, or seeing slides or photos. Their energies and inclinations

demand action – and where better than in their own school grounds. Education from the close-at-hand is what carries communication and power and provides the foundation stones and building blocks for the adults of the future.

Elsewhere is stated:

> We learn by touching, smelling, hearing, seeing and responding emotionally and spiritually to stimuli. We can reinforce the experience by talking, reading and writing, but the starting points have to be direct, personal experiences. Our intention is to give predictor experiences, and to expedite and give learning to more abstract and symbolic thought through these concrete starting points. The spiral curriculum is based on these early starting points.

'Hands-on' activity is considered essential, and the grounds are designed to facilitate it. The 'all-weather' paths through the grounds were planned so that 'children will have contact with the wild flowers and with the fruit, without disturbing the very delicate under-storey'. Around the beds are 'herbs and pleasantly smelling things that you can pluck and pocket, because it's something that you might draw out later on when you need a little bit of nose and mouth comfort'. The children scatter handfuls of sunflower seeds in the gardens, and then farm them:

> They can pull the sunflower out, take the seeds out of the head, pull it apart to see how it's constructed to get some idea about the detail. I know that lots of people don't like those ideas about picking, but we believe in giving children back their rights. Hands are the cutting edge of the mind, and if you don't put hands-on, and have smell and taste and contact, then you cannot actually move forward or progress. It isn't any good bringing children out here with their hands behind their backs. They need to have hundreds of seeds in their hands to plant. The result should be prolific enough for children to harvest in quantity and investigate the whole plant. The sunflower planting and harvesting programme is a supreme example of the seed to seed cycle.

There were enough sunflowers that year for each child in the school to have one. They had a sunflower jungle in the school hall, and had a 'teddy bears' picnic' where they feasted on sunflower seeds, margarine made from sunflowers, and sunflower honey. Sharing and cooperation are important principles underlying these events.

New opportunities are appearing all the time. In the ditch, rushes are beginning to grow and

> When you're talking about rush torches, rush mats, or reading the traditional stories like 'Cap o' Rushes', there'll be the means in the school gardens to come out and access the plant itself. Books offer vicarious learning – for young children, the direct experience is crucial.

On the last day of the Easter term it is traditional for everybody to make their own 'bird's nest' from materials which the birds use naturally:

> So you pick apart two or three old nests and you look at books or slides. Then you go out and you identify moss, straw, twigs, dry grass, dead leaves. Then you put these things together and you try to make a nest. Of course, the easiest ones are those made of moss because they hold together so well.

Many different kinds of life abound. The habitat piles guarantee hibernating newts, and

> There are niches for different forms of life. If we shifted this lot now, I could absolutely guarantee we'd find five or six toads. That would be enough for a group to have a lesson. You'd have to come out and find them first, but it's absolutely dependable. They would be handled gently, placed in an aquarium, and brought indoors. The children would have their lesson on living things, then bring them out later in the day and release them, so they return to their original habitat.

The children pond dip throughout the year, finding newts, toads, frogs, water snails, insects, leeches, dragonflies and many other forms of life. There are some 'remarkable butterflies, caterpillars and moths. The minute you get a whole lot of wild flowers, you begin to get a lot of night-time activity with moths.' They had set moth traps, so that the children could study them, being sure to release them afterwards.

On one afternoon, the local shepherd came in to wash the sheep. All of the school witnessed this, suitably clad in rubber boots and aprons. They joined in the hosing and washing. They felt their fleeces before and after. Sophie felt 'lots of bits when she rubbed them', Richard 'lots of dirt', Chris 'some twigs, and it was very scratchy'. After their shampoo they were 'nice and soft'. Others said, 'It stunk of dirty', 'I rinsed the sheep with a hose pipe'. Afterwards they wrote about and illustrated their experience. Alex (reception) wrote a page of emergent writing, but he read it to us with perfect sense. Apparently, it was his first attempt at writing. This was what he read:

> The water was warm and the sheep liked it. All the boys and girls thought it was good. They put in the bath took turns at squirting at the sheep with the hose pipe. The sheep was scared. The hose was too fast. So it just be brave and didn't scare it. It was nearly liked it – liked the bath, but not the hose pipe.

This seemed to us a brilliant attempt at a first story, which conveyed the basic details, the feelings involved (especially of the sheep), and some intelligent reasoning.

The dominant feature of the grounds is undoubtedly the trees. There are immediate rewards in terms of learning, and also a larger one. 'Growing a future wood is a most rewarding experience'. The school has a 'grow your own forest' idea, which involves all the children, and gives a sense of directly contributing to a small part of the planet. That very autumn they had planted some thirty trees, with each class group having six trees to plant. Sometimes they sowed seeds, pips or stones, but most trees were bought as whips or larger. 'That means you can get hands-on, and can help to dig the hole and all that sort of thing.' Children had been planting trees regularly for twenty-eight years. Some years, a class might only have had a couple of trees to plant, but in other years 'every child in the school will plant a tree – that's the nicest thing'.

Having planted trees, you have the right to enjoy them. For example:

> We always pick our own Christmas tree and we cut it down ceremonially, stand around it, carry it in, and decorate it on

that day with things the children have made. If you have the responsibility and the joy in planting, you are entitled to pick and harvest.

Ivy, holly and mistletoe are also grown and used in this way. The same applies to the fruit trees – apple, pear, quince, medlar, cherry, almond, hazel, chestnut, walnut, plum. Some fruits are eaten fresh, others make jam, jelly, chutneys; the rest are taken home. In September, every child goes out and ceremonially picks an apple, goes in, rubs it, bites it, and eventually goes out again and plants the pips, which also connects with traditional tales like 'Johnny Appleseed' and 'William Tell'. The crops help the teachers deal with vital concerns such as

> diet, methods of food preservation, experiments with salt, sugar and vinegar, the seed to seed cycle, patterns of weather and its effect, mildew and fungus, decay and death, symbiotic relationship, parasites, soil structure, annual and seasonal patterns, food chains, our dependence as human beings on the soil in general.

In other ways, too, trees are a considerable resource. There are trees 'to climb, to work under, to swing on. Their shapes, textures and colours fill the mind as well as the skyline.' They play among them, eat under them. Branches overhang recreation spaces and become part of their recreation.

They have planted trees around the playground and up to the school buildings, 'mitigating the effect of the prevailing east wind, giving colour and shape to their once naked boundary, and offering children eye, ear and nose contact with a range of living things. What the children view from the school windows and in the playground is a variety of pictures, changing throughout the year. It excites their interest, stimulates their curiosity, and feeds their intellect and imagination'. Above all, it's the *feel* that you get from it that counts.

The 'hands-on' experience is taken through from the input of knowledge and sensation – the initial sowing of seeds, planting trees, handling leaves, etc. – to demonstrations of its output – the making of books, plays, birds' nests even, and the cooking and eating of food. There are some magnificent bound books on display, all made by teachers, with some help from parents. Some of these have wooden covers, painted illustrations or beautiful photographs. They provide both a record, and a vivid means of reflection. Among them are 'The Coombes Potato Harvest', 'Coombes School's Stone Soup', 'Coombes School's Recipe Book', 'Porky and Brian' (about the school's pigs), 'Pumpkin Day', 'Making Pancakes', 'A Planter at Work: A Guide for Young Woodlanders', 'Megan the Sheep', 'Growing Food: The Seed to Seed Cycle', 'Cutting Down a Tree', 'A Bird's Eye View of the Coombes', and several stories. Other activities during our time there included a painting exhibition under the heading 'Our First Trees Are in Blossom', with pictures of quince, cherry, pear, plum, apple, medlar and lilac.

This close contact with the grounds, the application of all their senses, and their involvement in its development and maintenance, gives the children, Sue feels, a sense of ownership. There are no complicated rules governing their use of the grounds. Sue is 'very deeply influenced by the view that 'no one person owns land, or the past'. Through the summer and autumn they have days when the car park at the front of the school becomes the playground. The children are free to go into the wooded areas there. Compaction and wear problems prevent this happening every day, for you would have 'no herb layer left, and no regenerative system'. There was also a 'lot of fascinating caterpillar and insect life, like the hawk-moth, for example, which drops off trees and depends on a soft landing and an immediate burial to go through metamorphosis'. If the ground is compacted, then it can't go into stage two, and 'that's been the tragedy of a number of wild areas where you let folks go anywhere'.

It is a freedom, therefore, which operates within rules emerging from the exigencies of natural preservation. It is the same natural laws that give the children their rights – rights with responsibility. A school pamphlet asserts that 'an imaginative, rich environment which meets all human needs is every child's right. By working with children, we're assisting them towards the future which is theirs'.

The range and variety of places for children to go, to observe, to play, converse, sit quietly on their own, adds a further dimension to children's learning and development:

> It gives the children a new feel and a sense of ownership about many of the places in the school, and they don't have to play only in the same spot. It's so tranquillising for them. It isn't something that you can verbalise, but being surrounded by

beautiful things in interesting form has a deep effect on the human psyche.

Holism

For the Froebelians, nature study is a means to understanding the unity of creation:

> Country children grow up in an environment of farms and gardens where there is birth, life, death, life re-born year in, year out in a wealth of examples the whole seasonal rhythm of nature that mirrors the rhythm of life itself. We cannot recreate it in the classroom, but we must seek whatever instance we can to illustrate this cycle of life to develop an appreciation of the beauty, purposefulness and slow sureness of natural growth.
>
> (Hutchinson, 1961, p. 1)

The emphasis on holism is a prominent feature at Coombes. The teachers make no distinction between the learning environment inside and outside the school, and work to promote the universality of the learning experience.

The 'oneness' of life

In attaching learning to natural life, there is an aim of showing its roundedness, interconnectedness, patterns and rhythms. These are firm bases for learning. The whole grounds, for example,

> are meant to be something of a botanical clock, so that the production of small groups of wild flowers like bluebells, snowdrops, lilies-of-the-valley, come at dependable points in the year. So the botanical clock runs and re-runs, and gives you some idea in the two years that you're here of continuity and the annual cycle.

Projects in the grounds follow the cycle of the seasons, with festivals, special days, activities such as sowing, planting, picnicking, harvesting and dramatic events. The school values traditional celebrations. Mother's Day, for example, is celebrated by making bouquets of spring flowers, grown in the grounds, to take home.

The school's anniversary of opening is always celebrated out of doors as well as indoors.

The environmental aim is closely allied. Amongst these trees, Sue likes to think it gives you a feeling of 'being in a jungle' and 'the delicacy of the rain-forest':

> If you can begin to glimpse something of the fragile nature of the planet and about how some resources are renewable, and that, in renewing them, there is an adventure and a beauty, and the tying of the human to the rhythms beyond a single life.

The centrality of the earth is emphasised:

> Crops such as rhubarb are harvested by the children, who then wash, chop and cook it and feast on it before they go home. This is an essential experience if you're to understand that all food comes from the soil and all matter ultimately returns there. Children pick blackcurrants, squash them, look at the colours, know that that's the basis for blackcurrant yoghurt and Ribena. It's tying you to origins, it's giving us literally food for thought.

Sue Humphries considers it vital that children be involved in growing and harvesting food crops. They grow peas, beans, onions, marrows, pumpkins, tomatoes, artichokes and potatoes. Social education as well as technology is a central feature in the cooking, eating and sharing of food, some of which takes place in an 'earth and sea festival' which is part of the celebration of the autumn harvest. Eating out of doors is a regular occurrence with picnics, Jubilee street parties, barbecues and camp-fire cooking. Food not eaten or used at school may be taken home. Children thus witness at first hand the seed-to-seed cycle.

Processes are experienced from beginning to end. Thus, when the sheep are sheared,

> We start a wool workshop immediately that day. Felt-making is lovely. You can look at hats and other things, but you're also making thread and twisting fibres for strength and doing technical things with it. The children begin to understand that the raw fleece is the basis for carpets, blankets, clothes.

The school also has a textiles day, when the wool is washed, dyed, carded, spun or woven, knitted or felted. The children also make simple spindles.

Every attempt is made to ensure that as little as possible is wasted at Coombes. The sheep are moved every three weeks, and 'in cropping the grass, they're actually helping the wild flower production'. When there is no grass to graze, coppicing and pollarding provide some fodder for the sheep. The basic soil is clay. So they have dug a ditch and opened one end to give a clay bed. Children harvest the clay to resource their craft work. Seeds are returned to the ground. Thousands of tons of leaf litter swept up off the roads by Wokingham District Council have been dumped at the school and used for landscaping. The leaves form compost heaps which decay to provide humus-rich forcing beds:

> Dead animals are buried, and later disinterred for study of their skeletons. If children or parents come across a road kill, which is not in too bad a state, we encourage them to bring it into school. We then bury it and leave it for nine months or so. Then the teacher will exhume it. What we try to do is to match up a fresh carcass with an exhumed one. There are badgers, cats, foxes, etc., buried all over the grounds.

Integrating the curriculum through the environment

The holism that ties the child to matters in hand through the mediation of the environment is reflected in the way the environment also serves as an integrating and an extending force on the curriculum. A school pamphlet declares

> What we do outside at school feeds what happens inside and resources it, and vice versa. It has significance for every curriculum area, and in particular for language. The environmental work acts as a catalyst throughout the school.

Language is particularly important, the children being continuously involved in describing, explaining, questioning, experimenting and testing. They contribute their ideas to change, write about their experiences, sharing them with others. Flowers are used for mathematics, science, language and craft work. There are opportunities for historical and religious research. The system itself is the medieval one where everything flourishes with the 'weeds'. 'There's rosemary, and wode for dyes, and bay, all sorts of historical and medieval plants'. This year they made pot-pourri, herbal teas, jellies, etc. from the crops. Sue pointed to the lambs: 'How do you get across this metaphor of "feed my sheep", or "as the Father cares for his sheep" – the poetry of the Bible – unless you have direct experience at some point with these things?'

Through these means they try to give children 'connectors' with past traditions and age-old customs. They seek a positive valuing of the past, a link with their cultural and spiritual heritage to give meaning to the present. Sue argues that personal foundations are necessary for the appreciation of literature, art, music, religion, history, etc. Environmental work 'introduces and reinforces concepts of creation, care, order, love, families, birth and death, all of which may be ascribed to a supreme being'. A favourite quote is that of Sir Thomas Browne, 'If you want to know God, look around you. Nature is the art of God.' Staff at Coombes believe in the intrinsic value of ritual and tradition. Through these, children develop a sense of the school identity as well as a sense of self, and a feeling about the culture in which individuals are living and working. The traditions form cultural reference points for the children, and have the same sort of importance as rites-of-passage occasions throughout the year and through which children live each year. Rituals and traditions are vitally important. They are the image builders which children access.

Coombes is offering one way in which an overfull (Campbell et al., 1991), compartmentalised curriculum can be integrated. Hargreaves (1991) has raised questions about coherence and manageability in the National Curriculum. He distinguishes between content coherence (within and between subjects) and experiential coherence, that is learning as it is experienced by pupils. He summarises John Holt's (1964) view of pupils standing 'amid a bomb-site of disconnected bricks and fragments' (ibid., p. 34). Teachers are facing 'a massive task of curriculum co-ordination', and much of that is left largely to them. He fears that many teachers will render the task manageable by doing things in a mechanical way by ticking off checklists. Coombes offers a way of achieving coherence through bringing the curriculum to life. Partly through the environment, they are able to demonstrate the interrelatedness of subjects and their internal consistency, through methods that feature single subjects and through multi-disciplinary topics. They break down the traditional boundaries between school and playgrounds and between school and the outside world.

By regarding the grounds as a 'classroom' or 'library', and by promoting interaction among all these spheres, they contribute to a sense of unity. The world is the school, and the patterns, cycles, regularities and interdependability of natural forms of life present cohesive agencies for the curriculum. With the kind of environmental education envisaged by Wheatley (1992) it is 'far more than just a combination of programmes of study extracted from science and geography. It also encompasses moral, cultural, spiritual, political, aesthetic and emotional dimensions. It touches on all aspects of our lives' (ibid., p. 30).

Involvement and holism also find expression in the social life of the school. Where children are taught in a context which is 'very social, very involving, and democratically underpinned, it's likely to be absorbed and remembered and taken in as an owned part of what is being done to you'. Further, the social life of the school is

> the beginning of morality. That is what buoys it up emotionally. We come at that through increasing the social ambience in the school and people's awareness of each other. You create society in the microcosm in such a way that it isn't competitive, it's very much dwelling on the collaborative and the co-operative, and on our responsibility to each other. It's the only defensible morality. The most important thing we could do is to provide an education for a high social IQ so that children can adapt and absorb, and know the really pertinent issues, the multicultural and multi-faith issues, if we're to live in a world that doesn't see itself in such separate bits.

Inspiration and excitement

Motivation, stimulation, inspiration, confidence – all are generally regarded as highly significant factors in learning. The gardens and playground provide an air of excitement around the school, a buzz, that engages all the senses and keeps them alert. The involvement and holism contribute to this. Another contributory feature is relevance. A school pamphlet draws attention to the value of natural experiments:

Our study of minibeasts, our design and technological experiments (to move logs, make shelters, lift weights), our experiments with fire, earth, clay, water and sound, are part of the perfectly natural opportunities which arise from their outdoor setting. The populations of plants, fungi, insects and animals are the necessary elements for classifying, counting and recording in a curriculum which needs to be relevant, interesting, and, above all, meaningful to children.

In fact, it brings the whole curriculum to life. For example,

You come out in the Autumn term and there are hundreds of pine cones. There's a remarkable amount of fungus, beautiful fly agaric, for example, elderberries. That's what makes your fairy stories and literature come to life.

Egan (1992) has identified 'transcendent human qualities' in trees, and suggested how they can stimulate 'romance, wonder and awe' (ibid., p. 130). It is interesting that he should select the topic of 'trees' within the subject of science as one of his illustrations of the promotion of imagination in teaching and learning. Useful as his proposals might be, however, they do not seem to include the kind of hands-on experience that is *de rigueur* at Coombes, which arguably does even more to advance his aims in stimulating children's imaginations.

Sue Humphries believes that children need to be challenged, and to be given chances to take risks to stretch their mental and physical capabilities. The playground, for example, is meant not to be 'a prison exercise yard', but needs to be developed into 'a place of a thousand opportunities'

to encourage fantasy play, good social behaviour, the expression of motor skills, big physical movement – jumping, leaping, hiding, hopping about. Many of our playgrounds aren't physically challenging enough.

The playground is often turned into an arena for street theatre, concerts, circus adventures, jugglers, trick cyclists, marching bands, horsewomen and a range of musicians including African drummers, Irish dancers and the termly release of pigeons and doves of peace.

Sue feels that an excess of caution has led to children being provided with a sterile setting, which is against their needs. They 'actually need risk', and if it's not provided, they miss many opportunities for development. She cited the children of privileged backgrounds who 'ski, ride, aquaplane, glide, etc. during the holidays and at school'. The teachers also needed an element of risk, and this contributed to the excitement:

> It's the atmosphere that's set in a room – when you walk into a classroom and you feel that buzz coming out from the children, a sort of subdued excitement, or not so subdued excitement, a certain vitality, which comes in part from the teacher being vulnerable to experiences. We're constantly putting ourselves at risk in front of the children, and some things can go wrong. It's necessary for children to see that.

Promoting curriculum subjects

So far, we have stressed the degree to which the school grounds can promote environmental education and how they can serve to integrate the curriculum generally. We wish to say a little more here about how the use of the grounds enhances the teaching of particular curriculum areas.

The religious education curriculum includes the Epiphany experience wherein the children undertake a pilgrimage through the school grounds, visiting a number of 'inns'. Included in this exploration is the story of Roman soldiers, camels or horses on a trek, mock sleeping sessions, the relevance of light, the experience of religious fragrance, Middle Eastern foods, music, art. The Chinese New Year is celebrated by children making dragon costumes and taking part in a Chinese dragon dance in the grounds as part of a week-long celebration (see Chapter 4). Palm Sunday is celebrated by children and adults lining pathways and waving branches of cut laurel to welcome Jesus – children on hobby-horses and the eating of Hot Cross Buns is done around a large cross marked in chalk or paper on the playground. Divali is celebrated by floating candles on the school ponds and creating pathways of lights with candles in jars. The children make Moses baskets and models and float these on ponds and puddles.

Science is a major priority at the school, as we discuss further in Chapter 3, and use is made of the grounds to experiment with water

– bubble-blowing, making water travel by squirting or splashing and looking at reflections. Experiments with air are carried out through the making of kites, helicopters and paper aeroplanes. Work is done outside with parachutes, feathers, paper streamers and balloons. One year, arrangements were made for the landing of a real helicopter and a hot-air balloon. At some point every year, they do rock and soil studies:

> Clay is gathered from the school grounds and the children become familiar with the characteristics of their local soil. The smell of the topsoil and the smell and feel of the clay reinforce the learning. Earth is one of the most interesting topics to explore scientifically but it also has geographical connotations and figures in our environmental awareness programme. Firstly the topsoil is examined; we dig up squares of turf and the children pull these to pieces and identify the plants, insects and animals they find. They pull at the fibres to see how the herb layer is meshed together; they examine the strength of this meshing; and they hunt for signs of decomposing matter. They experiment with the soil in water to look at the sediment: they discover that there is air in the soil and they collect the small stones and particles. The clay underneath is compared and contrasted with the topsoil; we then use it for investigations into water tightness and malleability; we look at how the shape of a lump of clay can be changed by applying pressure to it; how its nature changes as we add water to it or dry it out. We make simple pots and a primitive sawdust kiln and alter the state of the clay, returning it to its rock state. The wholeness of experiences such as this, where clay is taken directly from the ground goes beyond knowing the facts so that you can be tested on them. It goes to true understanding and knowledge. Methods of teaching like this are part of an approach to life where children are making creative contributions to their own learning; the final stage in this unit of work comes when the children take home their fired pot and it becomes a reminder of the work; an icon.
>
> (Rowe and Humphries, 2001, p. 163)

Each year, a group of children build a kiln as part of the fire topic. They light it and fire their own pots. Science and art are drawn together in the way natural resources were used for William Morris designs from twigs, flowers and decaying matter (see Chapters 4 and 5).

Technology and the use of space is exemplified by their technology day:

> The children bring in toys and equipment to transport themselves and each other around the grounds of the school. Additionally this brings in investigations into wheels and gears. The work is further developed in the Autumn term, when the children are given the task of bringing in the heavy pumpkins they have grown in the gardens. Some of the pumpkins are huge and would need two adults to shift them; we ask the children to utilize a range of resources to bring the crop in unaided, undamaged and safely. What the children learn from these procedures is transferred to other areas of the curriculum: the pumpkins are not grown specifically for research into forces; they are illustrations of the seed to seed cycle. The 'transport technology day' is written up by the children as a writing exercise and the curriculum is taught in an integrated way.
>
> (Ibid.)

The grounds are useful for geography:

> Maps of the gardens are used to teach grid references and the children search within these for the clues to solve riddles or find the source of treasures. Translating the symbols on the maps starts where the child really is in physical and emotional terms; he is reading his own setting and recognising features and plants known to him. The maps are the best worksheets we produce.
>
> When the children plant their different crops in the Spring and early summer, they mark their planting areas on maps of the school ground; the site of autumnal planting of spring-flowering bulbs is similarly marked on maps. Cartographers have mapped the grounds for us and the children use these master plans as well as making their own. The very youngest children start out by drawing landscape features, then move on to drawing bird's eye views before being introduced to the notion of abstract maps and geographical symbols. It is by becoming thoroughly acquainted with their immediate landscape that young children start to develop a set of geographical

constructs and knowledge of their locality. This is teaching for transfer and we believe that fascination with maps and plans evolves from this type of early experience.

Folk tales, fairy stories and legends are full of lost boys and girls, and there are many examples of this situation/idea. We act out the solution Hansel and Gretel used when they were abandoned in the woods, and we see what happens to bread-crumbs and marked pebbles which usually have a spot of paint on them. We find parallel circumstances in other stories and we look at the predicament of Peter Pan and Rapunzel, Snow White and Goldilocks. This is one of the ways we integrate important stories into the curriculum subjects.

The eating of food is also an intensively geographical activity; whenever the opportunity arises, we ensure that the children have the opportunity to help to make and eat foods from around the world. For instance, when we are studying our contrasting geographical area of West Africa, the children help to set up a traditional three-stone fire in the grounds, they collect kindling and help to keep the cooking fire alight; we cook simple porridges or vegetable stews with rice and the children then eat communally together out of doors. The celebration of Bastille Day in July is accompanied by a French Breakfast of croissants. At Christmas, the children make a traditional Christmas pudding.

(Ibid., pp. 170–1)

Sue and Sue give some examples of how the core subjects of literacy and numeracy are aided:

We focus a lot on poetry as a vehicle for raising the children's awareness of the richness of language and how it may be manip-ulated by them to suit their preferences and imagination. Work on rhyme with the younger children often takes place outside with 'rhyme hunts'. The adults will have hidden rhyming words in the playground or along a pathway; or in the woodland areas and the children work outside to find and link up the rhyming pairs; or teddy bears will be hidden in the trees holding lines of traditional or other well known verse; the children look for the bear holding the first line, then the second and so on, until they put the whole verse together in sequence, often checking it against a written model they carry. Older children are introduced to the Haiku form and are encouraged to have a go at writing their own, often in our outdoor setting; in our bluebell woods on a warm Spring day; by the iced-over ponds in winter; or under falling leaves in Autumn. The sunflowers are a wonderful stimulus for creative writing, and the children's efforts are twinned with the published work of other poets to make a whole package of themed work.

(Ibid., pp. 164–5)

Art, craft and design, increasingly squeezed in recent years by government reforms, are important subjects at Coombes, and are enhanced by the grounds:

A lot of our art work is inspired by artists such as Andy Goldsworthy and Anthony Gormley; the idea of ephemeral art in the environment which can be recorded on digital film for the children is very appealing. We often work outside using the increasingly rich resource of our developing outdoor landscape. At Easter time, the children make patterns and pictures using leaves and flowers gathered from the grounds, and they put dyed eggs in them to act as a focal point in the pictures. Flower heads, leaves in Autumn, twigs, stones, willow gathered from our trees are used by the children in their 3-D work; often their artistry is set out of doors, but sometimes they bring in their raw materials and set up ephemeral art displays in the classroom or school hall. These are recorded in colour prints, slide images or digital images which update our intranet site. We encourage the children to perceive themselves as artists, and to make bold and large statements in the playground or car park areas. We give the children chalks or charcoal and ask them to put their images onto the tarmac or concrete floors. The next rain will wash away the images, but the act of drawing directly onto the site is very liberating. It takes us back to our distant ancestors who made their marks on the walls of caves and mountains; who set their petroglyphs into the landscape and whose work in this modern world is perceived as powerful art.

(Ibid., p. 172)

So, too, is music:

As well as experiencing the essence of concert music, the children are encouraged to be musicians themselves. Our music specialist leads them through a diverse programme with a strong emphasis on rhythm, tonal quality and composition. The initial programme for the youngest children is based on whole body movement to a range of sounds; the children learn to respond to a variety of sound with their bodies: moving to music is a natural way of exploring it. Rhythmic work using long sticks which have been harvested from the willow, ash and hazel trees in the school grounds, is another feature of the programme. The annual coppicing and pollarding cycle gives us sticks, which can be used for rhythm work. The children start their percussion work with claves or short sticks gathered from the environment and progress to the long sticks (often much taller than they themselves). They learn to work co-operatively to beat out patterns of sound, at first echoing the sound made by the teacher and over a period of time they learn to respond to musical notation alone. In this way, the children progress to fairly complex musical patterns as part of the intended spiral curriculum.

(Ibid., p. 173)

The grounds are used for mathematics with the investigation of sets and computation work with flowers and chalks on the playground. At harvesting children are involved in sorting, setting, counting, grading, weighing and estimating. Compass directions and map-making are brought into the 'beating the bounds' celebration. The use of sunflowers illustrates the mathematical possibilities within a holistic framework:

Sunflower harvest is an annual event, when the children bring in the crop. We plant enough sunflowers for each child to have at least one to pick in the Autumn. The children go out to estimate how many sunflowers are in bloom (dealing in fairly big numbers). At picking time, the children have some choice in the sunflower they want to gather, and the plant is picked root, ball and all. Since many of the sunflowers grow to two or three metres in height, there are opportunities for comparison of heights between the sunflowers and between the sunflowers and the children. The children take their plants into the playground, and investigate them mathematically, e.g.: how many petals/sepals/leaves? What is the circumference of the head? What is the length using non-standard and standard measures? How many seeds are there and what is the best way for counting and recording large numbers? The children make a chalk representation of their plants, and then they take the sunflowers to pieces, sorting and setting the different components. The flowers have cross-curricular purpose as well as mathematical gain; we use them for creative writing, for artwork and exhibitions, as a stimulus for movement, dance and singing and for geographical studies.

(Ibid., p. 167)

Again,

Apples which are harvested from our fruit trees are weighed and measured in a variety of ways: we do apple fractions by cutting the apples in half, quarters, eighths and then the children are asked to put the apple jigsaw back together again to help in their spatial awareness. We collect a variety of recipes, which use apples as a principal ingredient, and the children weigh, measure and cook the raw ingredients – and then eat their learning.

(Ibid., pp. 167–8; see Plate 1)

These examples give the flavour of how the school uses its grounds. There are more illustrations in later chapters.

Conclusion

The Coombes experience bears on issues of crucial current relevance. The first concerns the theory of learning and the teaching methods espoused by the staff. In its emphasis on involvement, activity, discovery, freedom, risk, child-meaningfulness, 'bringing the curriculum to life', imagination, holism, non-cognitive as well as cognitive processes, creativity, ownership, and so forth, it is in line with current constructivist approaches (Edwards and Mercer, 1987). These retain some of the elements of Plowdenesque child-centredness, but have the teacher in a stronger facilitative role. Primary pedagogy is currently very much a subject of debate. Within this debate, Coombes keeps strong faith with its beliefs, bases its principles in practice, and produces results to meet National Curriculum requirements and beyond.

The aim is 'creative learning'. So much learning in formal education is uncreative. Research on young pupils' perception of mathematics, for example, has shown that for many it was 'an activity which was simply an academic exercise divorced from reality', and that this view 'starts for many pupils in primary school if not before' (Hunter *et al.*, 1993). Where parents helped their children, 'unfortunately, by providing practice in routine rules and number facts they may actually have been strengthening the children's perception of mathematics as a formal exercise' (ibid., p. 25). The authors recommend that 'the links between the mathematics being taught and the child's life outside school need to be made explicit and established very early in the primary school years' (ibid., p. 25). The same point holds for other subjects. A wealth of research points to how knowledge becomes compartmentalised, particularly at secondary level; how groups of teachers struggle for status for their subject (Ball, 1982; Goodson, 1983) in the process differentiating from others; how that status can come to be associated with subject 'marketability' (Ball, 1981; Measor, 1984). These tendencies have been given a boost by the subject-centred National Curriculum. The Coombes experience offers a model for countering these trends (though not obliterating them), and for grounding knowledge in the real world.

Secondly, Coombes illustrates the importance of context for learning. This, of course, is a major point in constructivist literature (Donaldson, 1978; Bruner J, 1983). Sociologists, also, have drawn attention to the significance of the nature and arrangement of space for learning, and for conceptions of knowledge. Different contexts tend to induce different forms of behaviour from both pupils and teacher (Stebbins, 1970). For example, the traditional organisation of the classroom with teacher on a raised podium with pupils facing in serried ranks leaves little scope for other than 'talk and chalk' (Edwards and Furlong, 1978) and sends clear messages about the unequal relationship of teacher and pupils. Westbury (1973) argues that 'chalk and talk' techniques are dictated by context rather than philosophical conviction, context in turn being determined by resources (see also Hargreaves, 1988). In other words, it is a 'coping strategy' (Hargreaves, 1978; Pollard, 1982).

Much of this research on space in schools was done in secondary schools. Primary schools appear to offer more variety. King (1978), for example, found an infant school head advising 'Make your room an exciting and stimulating place to live . . . a specially devised environment which allows the children to be individuals growing at a pace and in a way most suited to their individual capacities' (ibid., p. 18). The contents of most rooms in his research reflected this aim. Coombes goes one better than this by applying this principle to its grounds as well as to its classrooms. This provides a living classroom, with strong roots, continually evolving, which provides more of a link to children's own knowledge than an inside classroom, and a base for a holistic future, offering integration of curriculum and of self. It might be argued that by taking over the grounds in this way teachers appropriate for control purposes areas that used to be pupils' private places. However, it would appear in this instance that many more opportunities had been given for pupils to be private, and for them to fill that privacy how they wished. Furthermore, the 'arrangement of props', as it were, is guided by a grander design than teacher control, that is environmental education in its broadest sense (see Weatley, 1992).

Chapter 3

The politics of appropriation

The reforms instituted by the 1988 Reform Act represented a major challenge for Coombes. In particular, the subject-based nature of the curriculum, the high degree of specification, the behaviourism of the assessment and the trend towards specialisation in teaching all militated against its philosophy. How has it managed?

The basis of the Coombes reaction to the reforms is one of appropriation. To appropriate is to take over, to use as one's own. In this case it implies that the school uses the National Curriculum to further its own ends, even though in some particulars its values seem diametrically opposed. This, of course, is not as simple as it sounds, and is not carried off without difficulty. However, in some respects the new requirements are well served by the Coombes approach, and it makes full use of that ('engagement'). The well-established and internationally acclaimed ethos and achievements of the school give the staff a secure platform from which to view developments. They have to meet requirements, but do not do so slavishly. As reflective practitioners (Schon, 1983) they analyse the new demands for what they are without becoming swamped or alienated by them ('recognition'). Comparing their responses with others aids the *identification* of their own values and beliefs, and sharpens and promotes the Coombes vision. In their adaptation, the staff seek, and gain, the support of other key groups ('alliances'). In what follows we examine these key features of appropriation: recognition, identification, engagement and alliances. Through them it will be seen that what was initially feared as being potentially damaging, has, in some respects, strengthened; through confusion has come more clarification; and from despair has come new hope and stronger will.

Features of appropriation

Recognition

There is evidence of intensification (Apple, 1986) at Coombes. It cannot avoid the pressures completely. Indeed, they are a considerable concern. However, it might be argued that the recognition of these is a form of appropriation. Teachers retain their reflective ability and are able to analyse the new developments for what they are. They recognise the threat of alienation that full compliance would imply. Their outlook is still governed by the old and continuing ideal, and they evaluate using its terms and criteria.

Many of their activities were justified in the National Curriculum, but, in line with experiences of other teachers (Osborn *et al.*, 2000) there is no longer time in which to do them:

> What defeats us a bit is the vast amount of paperwork. You've only got a certain amount of time in the day.

> Our teaching time has been reduced because you spend so much of your time standing back observing and assessing that it must have reduced the time that you're actually teaching them or interacting with them.

They had lost flexibility. It was

> a lot more difficult to say, 'Today I'm going to do so-and-so because I want to and because I feel like doing it, and it'll be good fun'.

This was not self-indulgence, nor did it happen often, but 'now and again it's so refreshing to just disregard everything and do something spontaneously on something that a child might have mentioned'.

A danger during the early introduction of reforms was that 'you're now spending so much of your energy on paperwork and form-filling and that much of our creative energy is being sapped, and that's a dreadful admission, but I think it's true'. There is a tension between being accountable, in 'audit' terms, to the likes of Ofsted (Jeffrey, 2002) and maintaining educational values:

You stop every now and then and think, 'What am I doing this for? I know that the child can do it, I know that the child understands it without having formal assessment', but there is someone up the chain who comes in to look at your bits of evidence. We now have to think of what evidence we'll have at the end of it as opposed to thinking mostly of the quality of the learning experience.

Their main grievance in common with many other primary teachers (see, for example, Broadfoot *et al.*, 1993) was with standardised national assessment. In the first run, in which Coombes pupils in general exceeded their standard levels, Sue felt 'we wasted three weeks – we all stood still'. They 'hated doing these tests' and it 'made their blood boil' because many of the tests were simply 'bad education'. They felt 'insulted' that they had 'no redress to analyse the tests and to come back and say "I'm sorry, this isn't working", or "this isn't suitable"'.

These teachers clearly have a conception of education that they feel is superior to that embodied in what they were at the time being required to do in the National Curriculum where the emphasis was on 'product and standardisation of the product'. In some respects, the contrast was enhancing their vision. It aided their sense of identification and unity in quite a cathartic way.

Identification

'Identification', therefore, is the second appropriation strategy. Comparing their own views and practices with those embodied in the National Curriculum and assessment brings the principles on which their practices rest to the forefront of the staffs' minds, forces them to articulate and hence sharpens their beliefs.

There were examples of past glories:

We spent an enormous amount of time setting up massive exhibitions of work from the children. We did scarecrows, where every child made a life-size scarecrow and set it in the school grounds.

I've been on courses where we were talking about the re-drafting of attainment targets, and 'food' is no longer in Key Stage 1 but it's one of the things which they can have as a common shared experience. You think of all the history that you get from time-lining, different cooking equipment and so on but they said, 'No. If it's not down in black and white, then we will not encourage our teachers to teach it because they've enough in the National Curriculum and that's how we'll leave it'. And that's a sad thing, isn't it? That people look at those documents and think, 'This is it!'

They rely on their tacit knowledge, which has been so strongly validated in their experience:

Our instinct is to keep on doing what we believe in and give the children first-hand quality experience in depth. We are dismayed at the thought of trying to implement something like science or technology or history or geography from a worksheet. We know how it can be done, and it can be real, and they can experience it, and we know we're doing the right thing. Every time we go out we see things, and some things we think 'Oh, that's good, we'd like to take that on board', but we also come back reinforced in our beliefs. The early science SATs, for example, were nonsensical – paper and pencil tests – that's not science!

The teachers were proud of their children's imaginative responses to unimaginative questions, like one where a go-cart was shown on a slope, and they were asked, 'How would you make the go-cart slow down?'

I had some wonderful, wonderful, imaginative and creative and very scientific solutions to this.
One child had a wall at the bottom, not for the cart to smash into, but just wide enough for the cart to go through but rubbing its wheels on the sides of the wall, thus slowing down. Another drew himself at the bottom and explained, 'I'm going to push it back up the slope'. Another felt you didn't have to do anything since it was near the bottom of the slope and would soon slow down when it reached the bottom. None of these reasonable answers were supplying the 'pull' answer required. Another question on the 'sun in the sky' had no compass points, no time of day in the pictures – 'it was just nonsense'.

The teachers here contrast their emphasis on process and creative reasoning with the objective approach of the National Curriculum requiring single correct answers. As with the old IQ tests, the more creative the children, the more likely they were to get the test wrong, because they could see different answers as being correct for very good reasons. The teachers applaud the latter achievement as good thinking, and decry the former for its blinkered small-mindedness. They felt that 'complying' was dangerous, to the extent that they would be in danger of losing not only control, but also their minds. It was the way to technician status, operating others' directives without question. Some who had run their in-service courses on how to apply the tests had been like this, being 'quite slavish about it, dotting the *i*s and crossing the *t*s and quite reverent about the stuff'.

Elsewhere, the staff identify the market-forces argument behind the government reforms:

> It doesn't have anything to do with quality, with what you're giving to the children as an education. It has to do with market forces, money, power – a real profitable organisation and that's not what education's about – it's about people, not commodities.

> You're not turning out a can of baked beans. You're dealing with the life of a child. You cannot impose those business terms.

There was anger, regret, sadness, but also humour, dynamism, analysis, resistance and triumph. They faced the crisis creatively, seeking ways in which they could use it to further their own brand of education. They had lost some activities and opportunities, and were being pressurised for what they saw as unproductive ends. But their vision of their own beliefs and aims was all the sharper.

The distinctive climate engendered at Coombes has been assailed, but not broken, by the government's reforms. Validated by years of work and experience, acclaimed by others on an international scale, it exists on a stronger and wider educational dimension than the government's efforts. This knowledge is the keystone of teacher morale in the school, so threatened generally (Pollard, 1992; Campbell, 1993). At the end of one early round of Standardised Attainment Targets (SATs) Carol felt it was depressing because I disagree so much with that, but I only have to listen to the determination of my colleagues to be reminded of why we're here and how much we believe in that. As long as we keep hanging on to that then there's a future, and that's what we're all fighting for.

Coombes can rescue and inspire new recruits. A student teacher at the school, now coming to the end of her year's course said

On a purely personal level about this school, I started the PGCE [Post Graduate Certificate in Education] in September very confident, very positive, very committed but until I came here I was almost on the point of dropping out, because every other teaching experience had been amongst people that are so demoralised. They just couldn't see anything good about anything at all. It was just having to match tasks to the National Curriculum and follow it slavishly, patchwork. I thought, 'I can't do this, this isn't what I believe in'. Coming here has changed that because we've seen how it can work. This environment has given me back my faith and has given me hope. I've found that the children are put first. I've seen the National Curriculum, which I saw as paper work in college, actually come alive for me in ways that I never thought it could come alive. It has shown me lots of ideas that I've never heard anywhere else.

A fellow student agreed:

We've seen that it can be done, after struggling through the winter months, not thinking that this is possible, to actually see it, and the children enjoying it, it's wonderful to find. We just wish our colleagues could have come along as well . . . The great proportion of people on our course have felt demoralised when they've been called out for teacher practice.

Another wished

I had a school like this when I was their age because I hated school. It was boring, dull, all sit at a desk and 'this is the work we're going to do today'. To come here and see the children enjoying it so much, it's wonderful.

All the teachers, in one way or another, affirmed their dedication to Coombes and its values:

> I did an afternoon's supply, then I did a maternity leave for someone and I've been here ever since. It's a very, very special place, and there is no way I have any wish to be anywhere else.

Others repeated this sentiment in a round of reaffirmation of commitment. The school's distinctiveness was its major strength, but also, in current times, was seen by them as a potential weakness, since it was

> unconventional, which is a word often used of us, but is not seen as a strength in the present government's vocabulary. It's seen as something that goes against the grain, and therefore is a danger and a threat. We were told that certain schools are being 'targeted' before any criteria are published, and that worries me a lot.

In the face of these dangers, however, 'the main thing was not to lose our integrity'. Fortunately, their main resource is permanent. There are times when they sound a bit 'doom and gloomish',

> but you've only got to take a deep breath and just step outside with the children and then you know exactly what it's all about. When you watch the children out there really experiencing and learning and developing all these concepts which are detailed in the National Curriculum, that's what it's all about. I can't wait till the SATs are over. This Friday we'll be having a drink to celebrate and then I think we'll get back to what it's all about – really teaching the children.

This research provided them with another opportunity for reflection:

> I think it's very important for us to hear what we believe from each other and you're giving us an opportunity now to just think back to what we do stand for professionally. By debating in this way, possibly nothing will come out of this for two or

three weeks, but in fact we're all articulating what we believe to each other and that takes you on a little stride. It's quite subtle actually.

The reflectivity of the staff is aided in other ways – for example, by the kind of reinforcement that comes from the enthusiasm and gratitude of others, as in this letter of thanks from a delegation from a local borough council:

> What an inspiration you are to us all. You would have been delighted if you could have heard the comments. They were quite overwhelmed by all that they had seen. We are now all full of ideas for a new Environmental Resource Centre.

The steady stream of national and international visitors and their own external activities help Coombes' teachers put the National Curriculum into perspective. Sue Humphries has taught a prestigious early learners' course in the USA. Sue Rowe has been to Russia, and is a frequent visitor to Africa. Both Sues and Carole have been to Sweden to visit schools. Their national and international reference set gives them both strength and vision.

Engagement

Coombes' teachers certainly found the National Curriculum constraining to some extent but, despite their reservations about the general philosophy behind the changes, they seek to be positive in their response, to use the National Curriculum and to use it adventurously

> as a baseline from which to grow not to become slaves to it, but to actually use it and adapt it in the ways that suit our philosophy and don't perhaps narrow our outlook too much.

Their science curriculum policy statement, for example, says:

> Each area of the National Curriculum Science is covered over and over again in a two year cycle: much of the science work at the school goes beyond the requirements of the National Curriculum.

And:

> The National Curriculum defines the range of knowledge
> expected from the children in Key Stage 1, and the Science Policy
> at the Coombes encompasses this, and enhances it. The
> statutory requirements of the National Curriculum are seen as
> a base line of knowledge and understanding: the practice of the
> school is to take children beyond the base lines and the obvious,
> and to give then a deeper understanding of scientific issues.

The renewed focus on some formerly neglected curriculum areas
such as science and geography was welcomed and

> When we do a big history or geography input we seem to be
> able to do it in a very imaginative way. We do it in a creative
> way, which doesn't take away from the philosophy, and as long
> as we stick to that I think we'll be fairly happy.

There were exciting things they used to do which, with some
ingenuity, they could still do. One recalled:

> a very important module of work based on 'milk' – dairy
> products. We went to the farms, met the cows, a cow came here,
> we made cheese, butter, milkshakes, yoghurts, and we milked
> a goat as well.
>   When I think of doing something like 'air', when we had
> the helicopter, the balloonists, the free-fall parachute people –
> that would be completely justifiable in terms of National
> Curriculum.

Submersion by the 'paperwork' is countered by the vision that
spurs them on: 'We think, well, we've just got to run with it this
time.' This is what Lacey (1976) would call 'strategic compliance';
wherein the individual accepts the prevailing system though
entertains private reservations. The 'compliance', however, is tem-
porary, and there is an ongoing attempt at 'strategic redefinition',
that is, to redefine the National Curriculum through their own
values. Sue has hope and confidence for the future:

> I actually think it's going to be all right. One of my colleagues
> gets worried at times but I keep patting her and saying, 'Don't
> worry. It's going to be OK.'

Another agreed, 'Stick it out'. One colleague, newly returned to the school, thought that

> The staff here are really good, trying to get to grips with what is required of them, and they're adapting it and using everything they've got around them to present it in the best possible way that they can. Had I gone to some other schools I may not have wished to continue my career as a teacher. Having come here I feel that there is a way forward for me teaching. The spirit in a lot of other schools is very low, and I don't think I would have that commitment.

The development of the school grounds still goes from strength to strength, as we saw in Chapter 2. It is 'a fantastic resource' for the National Curriculum:

> When people were implementing science for the first time they didn't have the resources, but we've got a living laboratory and we use it also for history, geography, technology. We analyse more than we used to, as you have to justify what you're doing, whereas we used to operate a lot more on instinct.

The National Curriculum, therefore, has not inhibited their use of the school grounds, 'In fact, it's probably spurred us on to keep finding things out there to resource it' and to integrate it. One example is the 'turf maze'. Work on this followed the suggestion from one family, who had visited a maze in 1991, the 'Year of the Maze':

> Our children wanted to know why we did not have a maze! So, in the maths room, the children started work with simple grids and grid references, and they made models with bricks. In their technology work, the children used the mathematical models and began to translate these using rope, string and furniture. In the language area, the children heard the story of Theseus and the Minotaur: they acted out the story: the children worked in pairs with a ball of knitting wool so that one child held the ball of wool while the partner unwound the wool and made a journey outside. He/she then had to re-wind the wool and retrace his/her steps to find their way back to the partner.

Other traditional tales, such as Hansel and Gretel with the 'hunt and find' theme were enjoyed. Historical stories of perseverance and problem solving were read, and the children could try out a variety of traditional maze designs in 2-D form.

Geographical skills were called into action when the children and staff had to identify an area of the school grounds large enough, and with the correct criteria, to contain a large turf maze. Scientific skills were drawn on as the children worked out how wide and tall the turf walls would need to be in order to be stable. They pondered what would hold the turves together, and the purpose of plant roots was identified and reinforced.

We enlisted a volunteer force of workers to help the children cut and transport turves, and to construct the maze. The maze has been an intriguing addition to the school grounds: it was the centrepiece for the acting out of the Epiphany Journey. The maze gave opportunity for every area of the curriculum to be called into action in an exciting and dynamic way.

(From the school's submission to The Royal Anniversary Trust Awards)

Special mention might be made of science, which is the school's forte. Sue Humphries and Sue Rowe have written two books on science teaching at Key Stage 1 of the National Curriculum, which aim to meet specified attainment targets and preserve their vision of science as a living experience (Humphries and Rowe, 1993a, 1993b). The books deal with fourteen themes, such as 'Earth', 'Water', 'Air', 'Fire', 'Busy Bodies', 'New Life', 'Death', 'How Things Move', 'Light and Colour', 'Kitchen Science'. They reflect the Early Attainment Targets 2 (Life and Living Processes), 3 (Materials and their Properties) and 4 (Physical Processes). The Coombes principles are stated in the introduction to each book:

Although the focus of each book is Primary science, the method of presentation is that of an integrated, whole-curriculum approach, where sharing, discussion and theme-related activities set the children on a course of exploration and discovery in all subject areas. The activities are high interest ones which help the children to observe, experiment, research and relate their findings to real life situations. The chapter themes are rooted in the context of day-to-day events at home, at school, or in the immediate environment.

(Humphries and Rowe, 1993a, p. 1)

The authors aim to 'encourage the children to be active participants in experiences that are exciting, interesting and informative. We learn best what we enjoy doing. The books encourage the children to do, to discover and to evaluate, to be true scientists'.

This was the aim of 'Nuffield Science', an approach that was popular in the Plowden era with the emphasis on children engaging in 'real' experimentation and 'real' discovery, as opposed to the teacher simply imparting knowledge and illustrating by demonstration. The approach was articulated as long ago as 1898 by Henry Armstrong. He advocated 'heuristic' methods of teaching, which involved children 'finding out' rather than being 'merely told':

> Discovery and invention are divine prerogatives, in some degree granted to all, meet for daily usage. It is consequently of importance that we be taught the rules of the game of discovery and learn to play it skilfully. The value of mere knowledge is immensely over-rated, and its possession over-praised and over-rewarded.
>
> (Armstrong, 1898)

However, Atkinson and Delamont (1977), in a study of 'guided discovery instruction' at a medical school and a Scottish independent girls' school argue that 'what appears as "discovery" is the recapitulation of the socially agreed nature of "science", "medicine" and the natural world' (ibid., p. 107). Typically, lessons would consist of 'mock-ups'; situations designed to represent reality, though they are not themselves 'real science'. Atkinson and Delamont argue that 'such types of encounter are always precarious: they require a degree of careful creation and maintenance, and the borderline between bringing them off and spoiling them is narrow' (ibid., p. 97). The two science classes observed in the Atkinson and Delamont research illustrate the dangers, one being 'stage-managed' by the teacher, the other not being managed enough and leading to 'muddle, confusion and anxiety' (ibid., p. 96).

The difference with Coombes' experiments is that they are real – using real materials on a real site for a real purpose. They do not recreate situations in a 'mock-up', and there are no artificial 'borderlines'. Atkinson and Delamont affirm that

The relationship between 'reality' and 'mock-ups' is dialectical. It is particular features of 'reality' that are selected and reconstructed to produce 'the working model'. In the same way, the model itself provides an interpretative framework whereby the reality may in time be understood. Through these 'reality-like' experiences, students amass a stock of typifications and recipes for action in typical circumstances in preparation for situations that are 'for real'.

(Ibid., p. 106)

One might argue that where the 'working model' is nature itself the correspondence to reality is closer, the pupil engages in more genuine discovery, the 'interpretative framework' has more of a unity, and rather purer (though applied) science is produced.

All the practical experiments and activities suggested by Sue and Sue have been conducted and tested at school. They include: digging holes and examining the soil, structure and constituents, life and remains of life in the soil; the time capsule idea; growing crops, many experiments with water; many experiments and observations of plants and wild life; 'life counts' and 'safari hunts'; cooking; composting (recycling dead plant matter); collecting colours from the school grounds; listening for and analysing sounds; pushing and pulling; flying kites. They also do large-scale experiments by starving the grass of light to make paths the children can walk on. Not all the activities use the school grounds – but they are the main resource. The young readers are encouraged to ask their teacher to arrange for the local council to dump autumn leaves in the school grounds; and when these have decayed into rich soil, to try growing pumpkins, marrows or sunflowers.

Sue Humphries talked about their experiments with fire: preparing and lighting a bonfire (with an adult present); observing how different things burn, noise, smells, colours, shapes, examining the ashes, using a biscuit tin as an oven for potatoes; experiments with candles, testing for light and heat; a visit from a fire engine (for which you need to plan weeks in advance); and various projects, including a candle vigil for Armenia and a candle walk for the millennium using 2000 candles. Again, the important thread running through the activities is that of life, in this case 'living fire'.

For Sue, the National Curriculum 'doesn't open things up so that you can move off. Things are so well tailored that the spontaneous can be neglected. The magic cocktail of the children's reaction is missing'. Sue believes in a basic framework that you can then 'dress in all sorts of garbs. You need control of the basics before you can begin experimenting.' Sue tried to make the standardised assessment tasks as active as she could, doing things like planting and gathering. Similarly, with the National Curriculum, she and her colleagues have found ways of meeting requirements through their preferred methods. For example, they sent home requests for moving things for their technology day on 'pushing and pulling', with bikes, skateboards, roller boots, scooters, sack-barrows, 'things with gears, bearings, axles'. Sue emphasised the social, as well as the physical and technological aspects, in the sharing of space and toys, and 'the considerate ways they rode round each other'.

This concern for social and cooperative learning is reflected in another book (Rowe and Humphries, 1994) which is a 'distillation' of their experience. This is a long way from the competitive, marketing ideology behind the government's reforms (Ball, 1993), but such learning, which receives token acknowledgement in the National Curriculum, still figures prominently in the Coombes approach. The introduction states that

> One of the authors' aims is to raise the level of co-operative consciousness in children: they want children to catch on to the fact that all human beings can and must learn from each other. It is a struggle to break down the competitive barriers which breed fear and suspicion amongst groups unaccustomed both to a co-operative ethic, and to sheltering all members. The common ground which gives children fun when working in teams and in small and large groups, and which fosters newcomers in the class, needs to be made explicit because it involves essential life skills. Curriculum provision for issues of race, gender and equal opportunity is partly covered through the playing of co-operative games and the involvement of everyone in a wide variety of social activities. It is in examining the outcomes of these exercises that the teacher is able to talk openly about fair shares, turns for everyone, vulnerability, risk taking and common needs.
>
> (Rowe and Humphries, 1994, p. 3)

Coombes, thus, continues to blossom under the National Curriculum, and itself to provide a 'cutting edge' for learning for other schools.

Alliances

In the face of the considerable new powers of the Secretary of State and the range of directives, it is not easy for a single, small group of teachers to withstand the pressures, to take over and adapt, on their own. They may have strength in collaboration, but they also need allies and support. Coombes realised this. They opted for a 'health check' – an unscheduled mini-inspection by two qualified inspectors and they reported that,

> You do a lot more than deliver the National Curriculum; you actually use it as a sort of board to leap off. That's not to say that it's not without a lot of hard work, and it does sometimes feel like a huge weight on your shoulders.

We asked the teachers if they felt their philosophy had been under attack and if they felt 'on the defensive':

> Oh no! That's the reason for having people come in to give us health checks, and to vouch for the effect of good hands-on experiences for children.

In other words, not only were they considered to be doing things right, they were not doing themselves justice in their accounts of themselves. This 'health-check' had an enervating morale-boosting effect on the staff:

> When you actually read that (i.e. the report) it was really quite emotional because to have it affirmed that what we're doing is going down the right track according to the guidelines that are set for a formal inspection meant quite a lot.

We mentioned to Sue an inspection report in another of our research schools where the philosophy of teaching was very similar to that of Coombes. The report was so critical, and indicated such a culture shift from previous inspections, that it drove the head-teacher to early retirement. That had been Sue's fear:

> I thought, 'Well, if I've been encouraging my colleagues to do things which wouldn't be officially approved, it's got to be my neck on the block'. We all felt very susceptible, I don't think

there was any one of us who didn't feel exceedingly tender about the whole thing.

The chair and vice-chair of the governors were invited to hear the report – thus enlisting the support of another important group.

Visitors and external groups saw the support of others as crucial in the survival of their vision:

> When people come in and say that what we're doing is good and important, they actually enhance what we're doing. It's so key, really important, and that's wonderful to hang on to on a day-to-day basis. But it's not always reflected in what the government or LEA say.

There has always been a strong relationship between staff and parents at Coombes. Parents have free access to the school, and every day finds many helpers on campus. A 'parent-helper' present at the discussion gave her opinion. She had left teaching just before the implementation of the National Curriculum, and was 'jolly glad to get out of it'. She had become reinvolved with education through her son's attendance at Coombes:

> I just think it's wonderful what goes on here and the way that they've adapted their ethos and their approach to education and tried to carry on within the constraints of the National Curriculum. This is a memory that will go through with me for the rest of my life: his first day at school and he's been cutting down sunflowers, and he was working co-operatively with some of the other (older) children and they were counting seeds. I thought it's wonderful that they can still keep some of the traditions that have gone on and find a place for them within the National Curriculum and present them in such a creative way. I think it would be a very sad day if anybody ever came in and said that this wasn't the right way to go about providing education because I think this is what education's all about.

On all our visits to Coombes there have been large numbers of parents present, freely engaging with activities and more than trebling the size of the staff:

> The staff are honest with parents, presenting their views and position to them hopefully, with good grace. It would be immoral if we were saying, 'Look, this is awful, and we're expected to do awful things with your children'. What we do is to tell them the truth that we actually teach what we believe in, that we adapt to what we believe in, that we adapt the National Curriculum. We do make them aware of the workload and what hoops the children will be expected to jump through, but we also assure them that their child will enjoy it, and we'll enjoy that process with them. It's a three-way thing that we'll all enjoy.

Their approach to the persuasion of other groups therefore, rests on conviction and consistency. They do not employ strategic manipulation presenting different truths to different groups:

> We feel we owe it to them and the children that we do keep them up to date with curriculum changes, and that we try to keep it as dynamic as we can. We all look a bit older and I've got some more grey hairs because of it, but we still try and do it.
>
> And the support from the parent group is mostly very reassuring, isn't it? The feedback we get is one of understanding and sympathy.

Conclusion

Coombes is attempting to integrate a curriculum whose contents 'are clearly bounded and insulated from each other' (Bernstein, 1975, p. 87). Bernstein stipulates a number of conditions if an integrated code is to be accomplished. There must be 'some relational idea, a supra-content concept, which focuses upon general principles at a high level of abstraction' (ibid., p. 101). There must be 'consensus about the integrating idea and it must be very explicit' (ibid., p. 107). The 'nature of the linkage between the integrating idea and the knowledge to be co-ordinated must also be coherently spelled out' (ibid.). A 'Committee system of staff may have to be set up to create a sensitive feed-back system . . . which will also provide a further agency of socialisation into the code'. And 'it is likely that integrated codes will give rise to multiple criteria of assessment compared with collection codes' (ibid.), involving 'a greater range of the student's behaviour', 'considerable . . . diversity between students and [taking] more into account "inner" attributes of the student' (ibid., p. 109).

Coombes has a strong 'relational' idea based on their educational philosophy, which has a considerable and acclaimed history and solid and secure everyday reinforcement. In the catharsis of the reforms, the 'relational idea' has, if anything, been made sharper and even more explicit in their minds by comparison with the National Curriculum, and their past experience. Their 'Curriculum Policy Statements' on each subject spell out the links between the idea and the knowledge to be coordinated. Their commitment, put to the test, has been strengthened. They have been further 'socialised into the code'. New recruits, students and returnees are soon inducted. Parents are incorporated into the 'collaborative culture' (Nias *et al.*, 1989) becoming a resource, rather than a constraint inhibiting integration because of their expectations of delivery of the National Curriculum. Coombes, also, are employing 'multiple criteria of assessment' over and above the limited and simplistic tests of national assessment. In all these respects, therefore, Coombes would appear to be meeting Bernstein's conditions for the establishment of an integrated code.

We have seen examples of the Coombes 'way' earlier, how it is articulated and the purposes it serves (recognition, identification, engagement and forming alliances). An interesting effect is how it works to transform and subsume other discourses, for example, recasting the National Curriculum science programme into their own formula, or rejoicing at the imaginative way in which their children tackled the SATs, while the assessment did not require them to be imaginative. Also, some of their established activities are considered indispensable for the 'charismatic ideology' (Bourdieu and Passeron, 1977), for example, the hand-painted badges which are made by the teachers and given to every child in the school about four times a year. These are made of wood designed in school and cut by a 'colleague's husband' from Lincolnshire, sanded down, polyurethaned, decorated, printed, then polyurethaned again. The iconography consists of animals, such as sheep, frogs, fish, or trees or plants, or symbols (such as hearts for St Valentine's Day) to mark traditions that 'we discovered in the less formal times. We realised their value and we've set our teeth against not doing them even though it scares us to have to do it because of all the work involved'. They are determined to continue because the badges are an important conveyor of culture. They are encapsulating symbols of all that Coombes stands for, part of the 'symbolic architecture' (Corrigan, 1989) that helps establish institutional identity and succinctly delineates its goal (Symes, 1992).

For Sue, they are important for

> Cementing people in a group, giving children folk art, giving children something of real quality that a teacher or adult has done for them, celebrating individuals, showing some skills because you're lucky to have them. They're a joy. The next-door neighbour notices it, and their friend notices it. It's an important marker and part of a social tradition at the school and a mark of belonging to this community.

So well does this work that parents will often remind them if their children are a little late in receiving their badges, or if they do not receive ones similar to previous years. The badges work as a kind of ideological currency, treasured and sought after by the school's clientele, and banked in the school's community account. As long as they survive, the Coombes vision will survive.

It would be a mistake to underestimate the power of the state and to deny the existence of structures within which schools have to work. Sue acknowledges that 'no school can sustain its beliefs and resolutely push out barriers if the climate out there is markedly hostile. Elements will survive, but they'll go underground, because at the end of the day you've got to pay the mortgage and get the children in. If you're ostracised in any kind of way, you just can't survive'. Another teacher agreed that, whereas the school had done quite well up to that moment at appropriating, 'there's always this sword of Damocles hanging over us'. Sue was confident that the school was well esteemed, but, as teachers, 'wanting to be tender to others and have that tenderness returned to you . . . we are exceedingly thin-skinned and that makes it easy for people to injure you'. Coombes to a large extent has succeeded in appropriating a curriculum and form of assessment at variance with their own philosophy – but nobody at the school is complacent. It is still vulnerable.

Chapter 4

Curriculum organisation and delivery

Coombes' teachers were presented with a number of challenges to their 'integrated code' during the 1990s. There were the demands of the new reforms, increasing cohort assessment requirements, the subject-dominated format of Ofsted inspections, parental expectation of attainment levels of achievement and demands for more specialist subject teachers in primary schools. Coombes is not an 'institution that is frightened of changes' (Sue Rowe) and they continually update their policies and organisation. They have developed a complex, composite organisation for teaching in order both to respond positively to the reforms and to maintain their value systems. It consists of three distinct entities woven together by termly themes, celebration of a large number of annual cycles and special events that punctuate the curriculum throughout the year. The curriculum experience is underpinned by a pedagogy outlined earlier that prioritises the use of the grounds and a hands-on approach to learning. Together, the composite curriculum, the themes, cycles and special events and their specialist pedagogy create a form of network learning.

A composite curriculum

Classes at Coombes were, in the early years of its development, made up of mixed age groups from 5 to 7 and the nursery. Since then the school has always had three specialist teachers, for physical education (PE), music and religious education (RE). The PE teacher is part time as is the music teacher, and Sue Humphries teaches RE. Children spend at least an hour a week going to the hall or the library for these lessons. Originally there were no formal groupings of children based on achievement levels. However, Coombes has always welcomed parents, visitors and school friends to work in the classrooms to assist teaching and learning, and consequently those children needing extra help have had regular access to support since the school opened.

The most significant adaptations in response to the government's reforms have been:

- the maintenance of a cross-age class grouping which acts as the home base for the children;
- the extension of specialist teaching to include PE, RE, music, science and language;
- the adoption of a model of teaching organisation similar to a secondary school where the children move from one session to the next by taking themselves to specific teachers' classrooms for 75 per cent of each day from Monday to Thursday;
- a school-wide grouping of children which is flexible enough to (a) allow the placing of children in groups that are commensurate with their learning needs and (b) move children within the groups when appropriate.

We can illustrate how this works by focusing on the timetable of a Year 1 child for a week. She begins the day in her home classroom with Sue Rowe, her class teacher, then moves to Gill's classroom for literacy, followed by Jo's classroom for numeracy. She returns to her home classroom for afternoon registration and then moves off to different specialist-subject-teaching sessions throughout the afternoon (see Figure 3). The last fifty-five minutes of each day is spent in her home classroom with her class teacher, as is all day Friday, when there are no literacy and numeracy sessions and no specialist sessions except for PE. The class-teacher days are opportunities to take part in special events or pursue projects determined by the class teacher.

Key Stage 1 consists of three age-designated years: reception age (4/5), Year 1 (aged 5/6), and Year 2 (aged 6/7). However, Coombes allocates the children to one of four groups for literacy, numeracy and the afternoon specialist teaching sessions. These groups are mainly age-related. The four groups are:

- reception – containing only children of reception age;
- Year 1 and reception – containing mainly Year 1 children but with some reception children who are more able;

Time	Monday	Tuesday	Wednesday	Thursday	Friday
8.50–9.10	Home base Sue Rowe	Home base Sue Rowe	Home base Sue Rowe	Home base Sue Rowe	Home Base Sue Rowe
9.10–10.10	Literacy Jude's room	Literacy Jude's room	Literacy Jude's room	Literacy Jude's room	Class Day
10.10–10.30	Assembly	Assembly	Assembly	Assembly	Assembly
10.30–11.30	Numeracy Jo's room	Numeracy Jo's room	Numeracy Jo's room	Numeracy Jo's room	Class Day
11.30–12.05	Handwriting Hall – Ann	Handwriting Hall – Ann	Handwriting Hall – Ann	Handwriting Hall – Ann	"
12.05–13.10	Lunch	Lunch	Lunch	Lunch	Lunch
13.10–13.15	Home base	Home base	Home base	Home base	Home base
13.15–13.55	Music Hall – Gill	PE Hall – Jenny	English Carole's room	Science Carol's room	Class Day
13.55–14.35	Extension Judy's room	RE Library Sue Humphries	"	"	"
14.35–15.20	Home base	Home base	Home base	Home base	Home base

Figure 3 A typical curriculum timetable

- Year 1 and Year 2 – containing a mixture of more able Year 1 children and less able Year 2 children;
- Year 2 – containing only Year 2 children.

This particular form of organisation is responsive to individual achievement and progress in that there is a termly review of the groups and some children are moved between groups to ensure an appropriate level of learning. The 'extension' session is also an opportunity for the teacher to select learning experiences that she deems necessary for the different age and achievement level groups that come to her during the week:

> We are aware that when we grouped the children, that a child who might not be very good with literacy might actually be quite a creative child and function very well in maths and science. We don't let the lack of literacy stop them from joining the higher curriculum groups.
>
> (Carole)

The size of the teaching classes is also reduced as three cohorts are divided into four groups.

It should be noted that space is found within the closely organised teaching programme for special events and community activities. Firstly, the Friday class group is flexible and some events take place on this day. If events or visitors' presentations have to be on another day of the week then the teachers reorganise that day's activities for the Friday. For example, if a visiting group were doing sea shanties with classes all day on Wednesday, the Wednesday timetable would be carried out on the Friday. Staff meetings, each Monday after school, have the week's organisation as a major item. The large timetable for the term, with all the prearranged events included is reorganised as new events and visitors are incorporated. There is a lot of rubbing out and redesigning and it is not unusual to see notices on the board saying 'Wednesday is Friday this week and vice versa'.

Secondly, the school may suspend the afternoon timetable and, on rare occasions, the morning core-subject timetable. Thirdly, the events and visiting performances are used as a resource for the specific teaching session. Listening to a harpist during a science-designated session, for example, would mean that the teacher focused on the science of sound.

There are therefore three forms of curriculum organisation: core subject sessions in the morning, specialist-subject teaching in the afternoon, and class-group teaching that operates in the last session of the day and on Fridays. In the first two forms the children are grouped according to age and achievement level and are taught by a range of teachers across the school. The class group consists of a mixed 5–7 group, of all achievement levels, taught by their home-base teacher.

Each form has its own distinctive characteristics. The literacy and numeracy hours are prescribed programmes, which the teachers overlay with the Coombes pedagogy (see chapter 4). The specialist-subject form is less prescriptive but retains an approach to curriculum organisation that has been a long-term feature of the Coombes school and could be seen as unusual for an Early Years school.

Dwindling time for non-core subjects such as art and music in primary schools due to an emphasis on testing and the prescriptive literacy and numeracy hours is now common (Galton and Macbeath, 2002), but Coombes has designated weekly slots of music, PE and RE for many years. The curriculum groups have one eighty-minute session each for language and science a week, alongside two forty-minute sessions for PE, and one for RE, music and extension activities. Whole-class teaching has always been an important feature of Coombes' pedagogy:

> We teach each curriculum subject together so that the whole group is experimenting and being adventurous. It is not a question of art being over there in the corner, or science being over there in the corner with an adult. You get much more spontaneous creativity because twenty-five and thirty kids have all got different ideas.
>
> (Carole)

Subject teaching, as part of a timetabled structure at Coombes, fits the school policy of encouraging children to develop identities as linguists, writers, storytellers, mathematicians, scientists, ecologists, actors and musicians. However, they have appropriated the specialist subjects to generate their particular educational values, even in PE:

> I work with small groups of children to interpret an idea in movement, which will tie in with the theme or the ethics shared

by us all. At the end of the first week of term, all the children and adult groups meet up to dance together. It is an intensely moving experience, which focuses on togetherness, and care for each other. Much of our PE programme concentrates on those aspects of movement, gymnastics and games, which highlight relationships: we use parachutes, balloons, feathers, scarves to encourage children in individual physical and social skills. Our concern is for self-awareness through whole body movement and for awareness of one another: it aims to set in us a pride and happiness about ourselves and for each other.

(Rowe and Humphries, 2001, p. 174)

The core and other curriculum subjects are studies in their own right but they are also integrated into each other's work where appropriate and possible. Music is a good example of how this works:

We play related music as an integral part of all our thematic work: Irish ballads and the Celtic Harp and Irish bagpipes around St Patrick's Day; male voice choirs around St David's Day; West African djembe drums and the kora in our African studies; handbells around Christmas; the lyre for Epiphany. We try to represent the culture of the local area, and music is strongly evocative. The whole school family has regular access to quality performance; we invite musicians into school to share their music and instruments; marching bands, string quartets, drummers, harpists, minstrels, steel bands, woodwind groups, buskers, folk musicians, balalaika players, and solo instrumentalists. All play for the children; talk about their specialist musical interests and explain the complexities of their instruments. We often play music as a background canvas for children at work; the CD/Cassette player is used frequently in all curriculum areas. Growth experiences can take place simultaneously and music feeds the mind while children do other kinds of work. We are keen on developing the aesthetic right hemisphere of the brain as well as the logical left side and music is a powerful route into this.

(Rowe and Humphries, 2001, p. 173)

Gill, the music coordinator, gives practical guidance to all the group and she leads the experiments to incorporate music into every subject. Other areas of the curriculum such as art, design and technology, geography, history and information technology are incorporated into the core, specialist-subject sessions where appropriate, or are present as major components of the themes and events that run throughout the year. They also figure heavily in the class-group sessions.

In these class groups there is provision for teachers to pursue individual interests. For example, Sue Rowe looked at nationality across Europe through focusing on different cultures, and Judy developed a topic on the art and craft of William Morris. This had originally been a light-touch look at designs in materials but developed into a major project with children constructing their own designs from materials in the environment:

> I have been caught up in this. It has encompassed the children's imaginations and sustained the interest of all the children from 5 to 7, from new children to experienced ones. It has been more successful than I had ever dreamt it was going to be. They ran with it. Children were sneaking off behind me to start instead of waiting for me to say, 'Come on, now let's sit, and let me talk you through it'. I would turn round and there would be children behind me doing it, and doing it correctly. It was a project where children didn't need stimulating. One of the things that I enjoyed about it was sitting with the children and talking about what they were doing, and listening to them enjoying this session. It is very relaxing and I also think they genuinely had a very strong sense of achievement.

During these times, teachers follow up the humanities and environmental education, art, design technology and IT are taught. The class-group time totals sixty minutes a day except for Fridays where the whole day is spent in class groups.

How have the teachers justified this composite organisation and what have been some of the effects on these young children and on the teachers themselves?

Changing the temperature

The specialist form of organisation, where children move around the school every day to go to different lessons, reflects a crucial element in the school's philosophy to satisfy young children's desire for novel experiences:

We are a whole school who fit together well but I also like constantly shaking the pieces and moving them around. I think the children gain from their experiences with every adult. That is why it is important to keep moving them. They can relate to many adults in this system and not only the one adult. You get changes of 'teaching temperature' all the time. I don't think they have much fear. I think they experience life in varying degrees, and providing the teachers nurture them it is not a problem for them.

(Sue Humphries)

The children experienced movements between lessons as adventures, as excursions to other parts of the school, to different classrooms, the library, the hall – and all unsupervised. These excursions developed independence, confidence and ownership of the school's space. They created an atmosphere of excited anticipation of something new and interesting about to happen each time as they set upon a timetabled 'journey':

Coombes School was interesting. You went outside and did activities. It was like an extra classroom. In other schools I went to you mainly sit at your desk. The school had got the amphitheatre and the maze. We did a show in the amphitheatre to an audience. You learnt in different ways. I learnt science and maths in other schools, but for science in Coombes we went pond dipping. Once we took a socket apart and learnt about it. We did much more fun stuff at Coombes than I did at other schools, like making Christmas pudding.

(Matthew, aged 9, past pupil)

Ensuring a constant flow of movement was incorporated into specific lessons where possible:

Sue's class is doing data handling. The class made suggestions as to what data to collect, favourite colours, favourite books, numbers of teeth, favourite food, what everyone is thinking about today, birth years. Sue says that some of these would have too many factors. She decides to investigate the types of music that the staff prefer – opera, pop, heavy metal, rock, jazz, classical. The children toured the school asking the staff their preferences and recorded the results on charts and on computer data programmes.

(Field note)

Learning on the move is seen as enjoyable 'because it is a learning adventure. The Year 1 children are looking for the alphabet in the garden. It is better than sitting on a table and it is an interesting game going around the garden finding the letters' (Sam, Year 1).

However, in this highly mobile learning culture, close interactive sessions with the children are still maintained:

Judy's class are doubling numbers. They sit in a circle on the carpet and they are asked how many biscuits they will need if each child has two. They count in twos up to 60 with each individual articulating the next number. Judy talks about her grandmother playing dominoes and she shows them some. They practise doubling some numbers. Judy and Sophie (a student) then move from child to child on their knees facing them and at the same time supporting them with warm expressions and gestures as they test their competence of doubling. The teachers are keen to get right answers but it is done in a warm and friendly way.

Some Bible stories are conducted with model characters carved out of wood that the children can manipulate manually:

Sue Humphries kneels on a carpet with the children in a circle in the library and tells the story of Jesus getting lost in the temple. She uses wooden figures and children sometimes handle them. Most of the children have to go out on a walk pretending to be the family who have left Jesus behind. They then have to draw a picture of either Jesus being lost or themselves being lost. They all draw quietly lying on their stomachs. There is only the occasional whisper when the adults talk to them.

(Field note)

Even the quiet reflective times sitting at a table reading, writing, drawing and computing appear as an active engagement, portrayed as 'today's' adventure:

The children exhibited calm enthusiasm and engaged readily – almost routinely. The varied and extensive curriculum entailed frequent changes of focus, seen as appropriate for the pupils' age and consequently they saw writing exercises as another interesting activity instead of a debilitating routine.

(Field note)

Their principles regarding the appropriate learning practices for young children are institutionalised alongside the appropriate organisation for the curriculum:

We try not to limit our thinking or the children's thinking by following a restricted and restrictive curriculum. Typically we target National Curriculum goals with lots of contrasting activities. They are often physically challenging because we believe that the whole range of developing skills fit together: we do not lock our children into chairs. We build into our daily programme elements of activity and physical engagement to help us model a variety of learning and teaching styles.

(Rowe and Humphries, 2001, p. 160)

These young children benefit from having opportunities to be mobile and adventurous but teachers also benefit from being able to work in different modes. For example, in the subject groups the teachers prepare materials and teach in pairs, sometimes separately, sometimes together:

You bring something to the group that the other person had not thought of that feeds you. You bounce off each other. I couldn't say how we are doing it, but because we get on so well and enjoy what we're doing collaboration comes naturally really. You share ideas. We are taking it in directions that the other might not have thought of. We share ideas and it gets you thinking about ways to develop and progress the situation. I love it. Because it happens so much you get to know each other so well. You play off each other. The children are sometimes able to choose between us, which is good for them.

(Jo)

Team work is undertaken primarily to implement programmes more effectively. It also encourages teacher development:

I pair-teach for both literacy and maths with Judith. Maths has never been a strong point for me, and when I told my dad that I was going to be a maths teacher, he laughed for about an hour. I really wanted to do it, because I felt it is an area that I feel slightly unsure of and I was really quite apprehensive at the beginning of the year, and I have had the best time. I have learnt so much, and Judith and I got on so well, and the children enjoy it, it has been fun. So I work with so many different people and take things from them. You are just learning from each other all the time.

(Jo)

Collaboration between staff is a central pivot in their policy of continually developing the curriculum and it is seen as a suitable role model:

The teaching group model conduct for the children: teachers collaborate, share problems and give each other feedback. The importance of giving is at the heart of a creative group; during the act of empathetic listening or of sharing thoughts, we open ourselves to revising and redrafting our ideas. Ideas are improved and kept alive by being spoken and overheard. Help from colleagues in realising the ideas, brings them into common ownership. The process of talking to each other is reinforcing, and we have also learned to use an intuitive mode of thinking where we brainstorm for method, content and delivery.

(Rowe and Humphries, 2001, p. 161)

Coombes' 'child centred' approach is not one that emphasises 'child-chosen' activities or construction of curriculum based on children's interests. Teachers choose the areas of investigation, bearing in mind the requirements of the National Curriculum as well as their own principles. The children have no control over the amount of time spent on an activity. In fact, their activity may be changed frequently, depending on participation in activities of the week, such as exploring the harpist at work, or helping to plant daffodils in a bank of land in the school grounds. The curriculum is a combination of national and teacher-designated priorities, albeit one in which particular attention is paid to the quality of the children's engagement:

We do not let the children actually take charge, but sometimes, they can change the direction of a session. Each time you do a session with a group of children it is different, because of the dynamic of the group. You might have two or three children in those groups who are creative and then you leave the session at a tangent leading you somewhere else. It is knowing how far to go down that track.

(Carole)

In resolving the tension between their own and government discourses, they have challenged some of the shibboleths of Early Years' education organisation, for example that young children need to remain with the same teacher for all their teaching and learning, and have developed a mix of subject specialism and integrated subject topic work.

Coombes operates both a 'teachers'-based' and a 'teacher-based' system within the integrated code (Bernstein, 1971). The subject sessions are an example of the first of these categories and the 'class group' is an example of the second, where individual teachers decide how far to develop any particular theme or topic. They have resolved the problem of possible insularity in subject teaching by ensuring that the teaching and learning practice is closely connected to the school environment and community and by encouraging individual and team practices. The teachers have adopted 'semi-specialist' teaching, advocated by Alexander *et al.* (1992) for the later primary years, because they judge it satisfies both the demands of government initiatives and the needs of this particular age group.

However, the composite organisation needs integrating media to produce Coombes' holistic curriculum.

Integrating the composite curriculum

We have already seen in chapter 2 how Coombes integrates its teaching and learning through the environment. The integration also takes place through themes, cycles, spirals and special events; the use of a specialist pedagogy involving experiential learning; and through the promotion of network learning, involving interconnected multi-perspectival and multilevelled learning.

Themes, cycles, spirals and special events

Coombes' 'relational idea' involves the designation of termly themes, a celebration of annual cycles, revisiting knowledge in a spiral experience and constructing special events, all with the involvement of the community:

> In order to make an authentic curriculum we use the community to set up a range of experiences throughout the year. We draw as much curricular clout as we can from these, and they form the base of our teaching and learning. Parents and grandparents are involved formally as well as casually in the idea, and we also draw on the wider community (craftspeople, authors, illustrators, and specialists in their field, musicians, dancers and the like). Many of these planned experiences are about children seeing creative forces at work. Seeing pottery and pictures produced, meeting musical instrument makers, exploring calligraphy and meeting performers with original ideas and releasing doves of peace helps us all to be a part of the creative process. There is often food to eat and a chance to share the occasion with twinned classes from our feeder junior school and our families. By involving a range of people in our work, we encourage them to make creative contributions to a curriculum where learning is visible.
>
> (Rowe and Humphries, 2001, p. 162)

Children are inducted into an experience of life as a matter of cycles and narratives through direct engagement with their environment, materials, people, stories and ideas. Repeated encounters with these experiences allow the pupils to develop their knowledge by building on previous encounters. Recycling experiences give new insights to children. Children's knowledge is reinforced by repetition of annual experiences and at the same time they are able to perceive these experiences from new perspectives filtered through new experiences and developing maturity:

> We are all in the state of becoming, but we never get there. The idea of the cycle, it's something that we are always talking to the children about. Every time you visit an idea your impression of it deepens, and your understanding is quicker and sharper. So I am into explanations about cycles, whether it's about mice

and cats or whether it's about environmental awareness, and the whole business about regeneration from decay.

(Sue Humphries)

The children rehearse the same Nativity story each year, and at each of four rehearsals they take different parts.

> As they waited for the rehearsal to start, the children skipped and jigged up and down talking to each other, feeling and comparing their costumes. They remained in their places on rugs placed around the hall and practised their parts by bowing and presenting gifts. They twisted and twirled the robes they were unused to wearing. Sue, the head, narrated the historical scene, as the children ate unleavened bread and lit candles. One of them was made from frankincense, the scent of which, they are told, reminds them that God is everywhere; and so the Christmas story began. The drama unfolded as a journey with a group of 'travellers' stopping at various places engaging dramatically with other players. They constructed the dialogue as they went along, some following the star (a torch) in the dimly lit hall.

They may not have remembered many of the details but they experienced atmospheres, tones, narratives and they played characters in the story. They brought their own interpretations to the creation of the event:

> We use drama a lot, particular in the history, RE and English curriculum. You can then twist perspectives around it and see it from other points of view. If you are standing in a different place or if you are coming from somewhere different, if your situation is different you might have a completely different perception of that situation. In November, we looked at Guy Fawkes as the baddie, trying to blow up the king, and arguments that he should be hung. But then we described the way the Catholics were being treated at that time. The children began to see the reason why such a terrible thing might have been planned. We think of things from others' perspectives, for example, the way we live our life and the way people in our twinning village live in Gambia where we support the Health Centre. They live very different lives because that is their

situation and their way of life. So they see things very differently. They have different values. All this is to develop creative thinking.

(Carole)

The Nativity is a synecdoche for the philosophy behind the Coombes experience and the school's belief in valuing the cycles of life, because it represents the value to be gained from revisiting knowledge. The teachers call this a 'spiral curriculum' (Judy), one in which children learn new aspects of knowledge as they engage with events filtered through developing experiences, concepts and perspectives.

The annual events that permeate the curriculum are not just religious ones. The children are told the story of the French Revolution every year in their classrooms:

Those who began the revolution had three ideas. One was about freedom, one was about equality and the other was about brotherhood. This is a general word, which includes girls and women. It means what we try to practise at Coombes, caring and sharing with everybody including the excluded, who didn't have rights and were not entitled to any liberation or any good things.

(Sue H)

A child who has a French parent was asked to stand up in Sue's class. She was dressed in red, white and blue for the day. The class discussed the French influences upon her life. After this the whole school eats a late breakfast in the hall with croissants and hot chocolate. They sit in rows on the floor with the French flag for their 'table', singing French songs, accompanied by an accordion. At the end they all stand and the 'Marseillaise' is played with those who know it singing with great fervour.

These cyclical events are part of the relational idea that cements the integration of the learning experience. Children anticipate each cyclical event as an opportunity to express their previously acquired knowledge or to pass some of it on to younger peers. This increases confidence and self-esteem. The knowledge to be learnt is not just delivered, received and forgotten. The recycling could be seen as a form of scaffolding knowledge (Bruner, 1972) through revisiting and engaging the child's ownership of the knowledge

(Jeffrey and Woods, 1997). These cyclical events gain pace as skills are acquired, as knowledge is gained, as enthusiasm is kindled, as relationships are established, as new heights are reached. They involve innovation, creativity, exploration, the stretching of facilities and experimentation with different media and forms of expression.

Carol and Jenny developed the light theme during the annual Chinese New Year celebrations. Each class constructed a large dragon. In the late afternoon the community were invited to celebrate the New Year with a procession and dancing around the grounds led by dragons full of children (see Plate 2):

> For the Chinese New Year, each class usually makes their own dragon tunic to represent a different theme for their own dragon. This year my class dragon had flashing eyes because we were doing electricity about that time. The dragons are based on the work of plants and stars as well, but they also light up. We try to bring something that we are actually doing in our basic subjects into the themes of the terms.
>
> (Carol)

The dragon moved round the grounds with appropriate musical accompaniment before going into the hall for more festivities involving the whole school and then into their own classroom for a geography lesson:

> Children can go out and plan a route where the dragon might be, and then go out and see if they were right, and then come back and plot it on the map of the school. It gives it a reality. Instead of just saying 'This is a map, where did we go?', we've actually gone and done it and looked at landmarks and looked at the compass, and discussed whether the compass is agreeing with what we think it should be. Looking at history as well, how they used to say 'Here be dragons' for danger. So it really brings things together which is real life.
>
> (Sue Humphries)

Jenny, coordinator of PE, explained how the children practised 'dragon movement' in PE, and how they prepared for the celebration. They spent 'six sessions learning the floor pattern of the movement, practising the different actions, and having ideas about actions, and then putting that all together for the final parades'.

Any week at Coombes is marked by one or more 'special events'. Many of these last a whole day. Many involve the community, such as the 'grandparents' day where older members of the community are invited to take part in a series of courses or offer training themselves to mixed groups of children, parents and community members. There are special events focusing on particular areas of the curriculum:

> One-day museums and exhibitions feature regularly in the programme. The school asks the parent/family group of all children in the school, as well as staff, governors and friends, to send in examples of a particular item (for example, chairs) and to provide some information about their contribution. They are then set out as a museum exhibit in the school hall; each exhibit is labelled so that the children and adults can access relevant information, and often the older children take on the role of curators for the younger ones. The children visit the museum two or three times during the day and the teacher tries to ensure that the maximum potential of the exhibition is exploited. Other one-day exhibitions have included Victoriana, pictures, clocks, laundry equipment, wood and shoes; all have a multiplicity of purpose in terms of curriculum value; 'for us, the important thing is that the children are engaged as active researchers and interpreters, using the exhibitions as their raw material'.
>
> (Rowe and Humphries, 2001, p. 171)

The science topic of 'forces' (see chapter 2) culminates in a day devoted to the subject. Children move from activity to activity during the day experiencing experiments with 'force'. Children fire syringes of water at each other to see if they can wet each other. There are smiles of concentration and pursed lips as their cold wet fingers press harder and harder on the syringes. They bring wheeled vehicles to school and push and pull them around the playground to test the best approach. They experiment with a series of pulleys under a covered way. They push and pull carpets, laden with bodies, around the hall (see Plate 3):

> One child rubs an eye with tiredness. They wonder what's going to happen next. They look serious and perplexed. They frown,

purse their lips, put fingers on their lips in anticipation and sometimes look worried as they watch the others. They tap the floor with glee, grit their teeth to make the effort, giggle as people fall off the carpets and grin as a 'a traffic jam occurs'. There is a cry of anguish as the children pretend it's hard, and of glee as they speed up. They are then put into large boxes and try to push each other around the hall again, experiencing the resistance of friction. They hide in the boxes, peeping out from time to time with giggles and cries of delight. The pushing results in many red faces.

(Field note)

Personal learning is accelerated by the intensity of the day and the integrating nature of the format. We have seen earlier how teaching at Coombes generates a continuous energy amongst teachers to embrace professional change. The openness of the school's practice to the outside world and its international-dissemination programmes assist the critical effects for the profession as a whole, of which this book is part. The themes, cycles and events are the life-blood of the organisational forms, bringing sustenance for strengthening practice and providing vigour for the curriculum subjects and class projects.

Coombes' specialist pedagogy: the case of literacy and numeracy

We have discussed in chapter 2 some of the features of Coombes' pedagogy involving the school grounds. Among the government's reforms, the introduction of the literacy and numeracy hours presented a particularly strong challenge to Coombes because of the degree of prescription, especially in the former, which seemed to leave little room for teachers' own variations. How, then, have teachers attempted to appropriate these areas and how successful have they been in integrating them within their own curriculum?

Trying to meet both the government's and Coombes' programmes in the early stages was exhausting work. Jo was up till 'eleven at night, making menus and doing things to make it fun and to make it an experience'. Carole had 'never been so tired'. However, they saw opportunities in the programmes. Carol was 'so excited about the numeracy hour; I think it is wonderful because I always believed in teaching maths like that. I also used to love teaching phonics, particularly to my less able children'. The rationalising benefits were also appreciated:

> It has given us a chance to refine what we have been doing and to ensure that we are doing pretty similar things. We are now teaching phonics in similar ways even though as you go through the age band, there is a progression. I think the only way we can teach phonics is in a highly structured way.
>
> (Sue Rowe)

Though daunted to begin with, 'We did it within the school's value system, and put the school stamp on it, and made it ours' (Carole). Coombes' teachers have adjusted their organisation, using their environment, their specific skills, and emphasising a hands-on approach. Phonics teaching is reinforced with singing, dancing, puppetry and eating. The children internalise the *ee* and *ea* phonemes by *ea*ting gr*ee*n beans and p*ea*rs or smelling sw*ee*t p*ea*s. They find the bay trees and take the l*ea*ves from the tree, and put them in their pockets for a fragrant reminder during the day. In ways like these, the programme becomes rooted in the real world, rather than being in the abstract or paperbound.

Towards the end of its first year of operation, the literacy-hour evaluator from the local education authority visited the two reception classes. After observing the classes,

> She just smiled, put her thumbs up and said '*Super!*' She was pleased with the activities, with the actions to the songs. She said the children were so motivated. Every single child was singing which doesn't always happen. It was a very positive feedback. I was so relieved.
>
> (Gill)

As seen in chapter 2, the grounds are used for core-subject work:

> We're doing a detective hunt tomorrow. The children love it. We hide a set of letters in an envelope and seal it up. The rest of the alphabet letters are spread around the garden, some hanging from trees, others hidden behind logs and plants. They go out with their check sheets with all the alphabet letters on it and tick them off each time they find a letter. They've got to find all the letters and tick them off because six of them are

missing. We then ask the children, 'Which detective has worked out what letters were not put outside but were in the sealed envelope?' The children are so excited to see if they have got the letters right as we take them out of the envelope. We then ask them, 'Why did we hide these letters?' and they suddenly realise that the letters can be rearranged to make a word.

(Jo; see Plate 4)

Each activity often has a problem for the children to solve:

Last week I had made up a dragon story with the children as shared writing. I then typed out some of the sentences but I did not put in any full stops or capital letters. I then said to the children, 'I've written out the story. You can paste in your books. It's really good.' They were all very excited. And then one child said, 'You haven't put a full stop at the end of the sentence.' So I asked him to use my red pen to put it in so that I would remember to change it. Then another child said, 'Why hasn't Poko got a capital letter if that is his name?' So they came up to the board and put right all my problems I had got wrong.

(Gill)

Pairs of children in Carole's class reviewed each other's story books and discussed the ways in which they made their stories interesting. They were encouraged to make suggestions as to how to improve the content and the presentation.

Coombes' teachers argue that basic (and necessary) writing skills can be conveyed in a variety of ways that are age-appropriate, and not just through paper and pencil exercises. The children thus refine their handwriting skills by practising on table-tops with shaving foam, chocolate mousse or talcum powder. They use large chalks on the playground and pathways, or paintbrushes dipped in water on the outside walls. They learn about sentence structure, full stops, capital letters, commas, question marks and speech marks, by becoming 'human sentences'. Each child will be given a word or component part of the sentence, and they are asked to rearrange themselves into a complete sentence for another group of children to read and check. 'It is through playing with these writing conventions that children begin to understand them' (Rowe and Humphries, 2001, p. 165).

It has been argued that making mistakes and being able to reformulate constructions quickly is an essential aspect of learning (Craft, 2002):

> There was another group out in the porch with shaving foam and a parent and they had to write the sounds in the foam. They also then wrote names in the foam. If they got them wrong it didn't matter, they just rubbed them out and started again.
>
> (Gill)

The approach encourages 'a slight element of risk, and we perceive this to be essential if the creative approach to teaching and learning is to be maintained and taken forward' (Rowe and Humphries, 2001, p. 161).

Learning through games was developed using popular practices making them relevant. 'They had a pile of words for "word football". They turned over the top one and if they got it right they moved one step towards the goal. If they didn't get it right their opponent had a go' (Gill).

Exploring the connections between music and literacy was popular. Gill, the music specialist, composed songs driving back from Sainsbury's:

> We then sang the alphabet song, but we did it with actions so the children concentrated on the actions as well as the letters. So their alphabet singing becomes inbuilt. It becomes automatic. We do it without clapping first of all so they are thinking of the letters and then with actions. They know their alphabet order through singing it. They concentrate on the actions but they don't stop singing. We can look at them and know that they know it very well. We can do it four or five times with different actions and they are still asking for more. They all know their alphabet including the 4-year-olds. They sing it confidently. I suppose it is from rote learning because they know the rhythm.
>
> (Gill)

But there is a lot of creativity in it:

> They always have to make up their own actions. They make up their own rhythms. Some groups have to write to their own

rhythm patterns in musical notation. It has helped in literacy. There is a similarity with beats and syllables. They do it in music and so they have the grounding when they do it in literacy.

(Jo)

There were many other ways of exploiting connections. Teachers used a 'Joseph coat of many colours' to investigate words with an *oa* sound. They made hand puppets, for example a *fr*og, to represent particular digraphs; the children used them creatively to read 'for them'. They regularly brought in something for the children to eat related to that week's sound, for example, *m*altesers and brown *br*ead with *Br*amble jelly and they encouraged the children to write letter sounds and words in coloured chalks on the playground. Children are given opportunities to take ownership of a story by adding to it:

> Judy works with the story 'Stone Soup' in which a charlatan persuades a community, who are portrayed as being very mean, that he can make soup from a stone in order to make them part with their money. There are pictures on each page but no bubbles coming from the characters' mouths. Children contribute to the story and argue as Judy pauses while telling the story: 'It could be a castle'; 'There's a fire'; 'It hasn't got a fire'; 'That person is not saying anything'; 'I think that there are matches in the yellow box'; 'They've got red faces'; 'That one's laughing so he's not so mean'; 'They got a stone, cut it in half and got some others and mixed them up until it got gooey and mixed it round and added some carrots and cream'.

Children also learn from each other about how to develop their language skills and structures. Ray constructed some 'dens' in her classroom and small groups of children constructed stories together hidden under blankets and covers after she had started them off with an idea and given them some artefacts to assist them:

> I grouped the children in a particular way, because I wanted them to be dynamic, and I wanted them to work together, to give each other ideas. They came up with far more interesting stories than if they were doing it completely on their own. The children who found it harder to structure stories learned from the children who were very able at expressing themselves.

(Ray)

They also developed the children's critical capacities by encouraging peer evaluation, such as reviewing each other's written work:

> It's important to encourage their independence. They can share views and what materials they used. It is good for children to get together with other children and discuss their work as opposed to the teachers always discussing it with them.
>
> (Jo)

The literacy programme involves a lot of technical language, such as parts of speech. However, teachers did not flinch from engaging the children with these terms. According to Carol, the children 'loved it':

> It is boring having to sit down for an hour. But I like sitting on the carpet having some really good books with dragons when the teacher is reading to us. I like literacy when we learn about adjectives and nouns. I hate sitting there and doing nothing.
>
> (Russell, Year 2)

The teachers at Coombes sought to embed technical skills within a meaningful framework. One way is through a project:

> William Morris lived hundred years ago and liked the country-side. It was beautiful, peaceful and lovely and he liked of the birds singing. He wanted to be a minister and he went to college. One day he didn't want to be a minister any more. He had met Byrne Jones and they had gone to be ministers together. Jones went on to be a pre-Raphaelite. A pre-Raphaelite is an artist. William was an architect who designed buildings then William became a pre-Raphaelite. There only was one finished picture of his and he decided to become a designer. He put his paintings on things and used wood blocks. One block was so heavy it took two men to lift it. Only the rich people could afford his designs that he wanted the poor people to have them to. He got his designs from the countryside, the moors, trees, leaves, birds and flowers. He made carved furniture. His designs for curtains and cushions are still popular today. Sometimes he printed straight on to the walls. There is a stained glass window of Byrne Jones and you can still see it today in a church in the East Hampstead.
>
> (Abigail, Year 2)

The teachers argue that the mechanics of writing only produce good writing if there is a relevant context for the learner:

> Knowledge about how the parts of language work and fit together is very necessary, but mastery of this and spelling does not produce good writing. A writer struggles to shape experiences through written expressions and creating a story or poem about something that has happened in someone else's world, will not bring the self-discovery of a personal experience. When a writer uses words to shape and explain experiences to himself and others, he is caught in the process of creative release which depends on his thinking and helps his self-discovery. The Writer's Workshop approach which came from the USA (specifically Donald Graves) puts writing beyond the awkward targets of punctuation, syllabifying and spelling and treats all writers as authors. This method teaches the mechanical side of language as the children liberate and respond to their 'inner voice'. When young writers become inhibited they stop exercising this inner voice and fall back on words they can spell and towards the dullest, safest expressions. We believe in the 'children as authors' approach, but via the National Curriculum we are also giving the children a thorough grounding in the mechanics of writing.
>
> (Rowe and Humphries, 2001, p. 164)

How, then, did Coombes approach the writing SAT, which they admitted was the hardest section for their young children? They involved the children imaginatively and used the environment. For example, immediately prior to the 2001 SATs writing exercise, Sue and Carol told the story of the Pied Piper of Hamlyn by 'role playing' the story using artefacts such as a cloth rat and some hats. They gradually drew the children into the story in the classroom to take the parts of the rats and the children. After trailing round the school grounds following the 'piper', half the class was led to 'cave' in the playground while the 'townspeople' were left to console each other. The children then did their writing SAT in the classroom having been asked to retell the story as one of the rats or one of the children.

Fisher and Lewis (1999) found that the most effective teaching of literacy among their sample of small rural schools was well paced, discursive, interactive, confident and ambitious. They also draw the contrast between teaching as a technical activity, where pedagogy is specified, and teaching as a professional activity, where teachers have pedagogical flexibility among a broad repertoire of methods. The latter has strong support in general as a feature of effective teaching (see, for example, Alexander, 1992; Alexander *et al.*, 1992; Strong, 2002).

Research has shown that many teachers feel that they have benefited from the strategy (Strong, 2002) and Coombes' teachers are also open to the benefits:

> I feel that the children focusing on literacy skills in a very specific way for an hour a day each week obviously has an ongoing benefit in terms of repetition and consolidation. It has informed their writing, their spelling has improved and handwriting has improved as well.
>
> (Carol)

The same 'reality' approach applies to the mathematics programme. In looking at the concept of mass (weight), the children collect a number of items which all weigh one kilogram. Boxes of sugar, closed containers of water, bags of tinned goods, baskets of stones are collected in the classroom, and the children pick up different items and get the 'feel' of a kilogram. They walk a measured distance holding a kilogram in each hand and chart and discuss the importance of handles, straps and the shape of containers for ease of carrying:

> Moving weights is a show of strength; the critical start to measuring mass is the hand/eye/body co-ordination needed to lift things. Until you start lifting, you cannot have a concept of mass – appearance will tell you nothing; our approach means that the children remember through their arms and legs.
>
> (Rowe and Humphries, 2001, p. 167)

When a large crane was on site, putting a roof on to a new classroom, the children observed the crane at work and discussed its weight-bearing ability and capacity. They talked with the crane operator, and got a glimpse of how a crane works to lift heavy weights over distance and obstacles, 'The children perceived the information in a real-world setting and it makes sense to them' (ibid.).

One of the school traditions is to make Christmas puddings for the school's Christmas dinner, and studies are undertaken into the cost of preparing the puddings:

> The children have to follow a recipe, and are immersed in all the language of food preparation (cut, chop, squeeze, beat, stir, blend, grate, mix etc.) as well as in the mathematical complexity of following a recipe and making a finished product from a variety of raw ingredients. They undertake all the preparation and mixing and the proof of the pudding is always in the eating! As well as being a strongly mathematical focus, these activities are language rich, and also deal with history (Little Jack Horner) and geography (where do the ingredients come from?) We plot the places of origin on a world map and discuss why different produce comes from different parts of the world. We research different recipes for Christmas puddings and look for similarities and differences. We may go on to undertake studies into the cost of preparing the puddings: every year a group of children are taken to the nearby supermarket to do the shopping and they compare costs of different ingredients. The children have to pay for their purchases with real money, and check that they have the correct change. Upon return to school, they have to divide the ingredients up between the six classes and ensure that each class has precisely what it needs to make Christmas puddings.
>
> (Ibid., p. 168)

Throughout the year, there are reliable opportunities for data-handling exercises which are based on real-life experiences for the children; for instance, on Shrove Tuesday, they make pancake batter, cook pancakes and choose one of five or six toppings for their own pancake. The children record their preferences back in the classroom, using conventional bar charts or histograms and also undertake simple statistical analyses using ICT software:

> After researching all the teacher's musical preferences with a school survey, the children are then asked about the data. How many people preferred rock to jazz? How did you work it out? Find the difference between classical and heavy metal? Can anyone explain how to do it?
>
> (Field note)

After lambing time, the children propose and vote for names for the lambs which have been born. 'We aim for the feel of a genuine "general election" complete with voting papers, booths and a Returning Officer. The intensely mathematical nature this exercise also gives us the opportunity to discuss civics and politics with the children' (Rowe and Humphries, 2001, p. 168).

The children were asked to compare the results of first-past-the-post voting (one person, one vote) and a proportional voting system (where the children are given a number of points to award as they wish between contenders). Voting for a favourite greetings card, breakfast cereal, type of bread, or type of apple compares the systems. The results (which are often quite different, despite such a small sample) are discussed and the children try to explain the differences. Further examples of maths activities are given in other chapters.

SATs results at Coombes for the years 1997–2001 show that they are broadly in line with the national average in literacy and above average for maths. Teacher-assessed science shows above-average levels achieved. Results for 2001 also show an improvement in literacy and science over 2000, with maths about the same as the previous year. However, maths was at a high point in 2000 with of 94 per cent of Year 2 children reaching level two, which is the average target level for this age group (Coombes, 2002). This is not enough for Coombes' teachers, who see their pupils as developing individuals, not as products that can be packaged for greater appeal, 'I don't think you can raise standards every year. You have got to look beyond this to children reaching 18 years, a lifelong attitude. It is what is in their hearts; that is what makes us different. It gives us the ability to understand other people' (Sue Humphries).

They pleaded, not for a rejection of SATs, but for a broadening of the assessment system:

> The children are being connected to wider artistic concerns, work concerns and spiritual concerns. They are learning other things as well as the National Curriculum. We are nursing the side of the child that is going to be emphatic, imaginative and tolerant.
>
> (Sue Humphries)

Network learning

Coombes' teachers see the learning experience as a maze of many entrances and exits involving many different but connected perspectives. Teachers aim to draw children into the complexities and connecting threads of the learning experience, and to enable them to master different codes and to develop confidence in finding their way round such networks. What matters is not just the substantive knowledge but the maze-like structure of the knowledge and the interdependence of its many different parts and forms. Coombes' teachers explore light, for example, in terms of spirituality, religion, growth, energy, electricity, ritual and dance. Phonics as language phonemes are eaten, sung about, danced, found in the environment and associated with playing detective.

Coombes specialises in experiences that are open to the net-like structures of knowledge and the multiple perspectives that make up that knowledge. The Irish project, which happens every year, in the week of St Patrick's Day, provides a good example. The children begin the week by hearing about some of the myths and legends associated with Ireland. This aspect lent itself to literacy work:

> We are doing the story of Finn McCaul. The children are asked to think of a giant and list its characteristics. It's 'ugly, friendly, cross, mean'. 'Mine is so kind', 'beautiful and sharp toothed'. 'Kind of fat, funny, helpful with an eye patch and a wooden leg', 'polite with good eyesight', 'it's grumpy, loving, rickety, its teeth are as sharp as knives, plump', 'we've already got plump – it means fat (Sue supports the contribution), a voice like a dragon with rotten teeth'.

Sue then told them about some Irish practices that have become legends. The children use their imaginations and their own life experience to interpret them:

> We have got money in our shoes. Miss Rowe gave it to us. If you keep it in your shoe all night and all day you might get rich and your shoe might be full of money. My dad might think I have taken it out of his pot but it is mine. This is what leprechauns do. A leprechaun came into my room and put my pony in my bed and I put it back on my windowsill.
>
> (Teresa, Year 1)

The next morning children peeled and cooked potatoes in the classroom. They ate them with salt and onions and some cabbage. This activity included some maths and cooking decisions as well as some collaborative experiences. Gradually, children were finding their way round the maze of Irish life, history and culture. At the end of the morning Sue decided to take the class out to collect some greenery for a classroom display of the Irish colour, which was displayed on a table in the classroom covered with green fabric:

> The evergreen conifers, holly, ivy, limes, sycamore, ash, hazel were complemented with greens from bushes and shrubs. A child suggested that she sit on a chair on the display as the 'green queen' and the children carefully draped the leaves and branches over her until she was entirely covered and had a suitable green crown. The children then took photographs, choosing their preferred perspective.
>
> (Field note)

Later on in the day the children were asked to make up stories relating to Irish culture:

> Once there lived two friends and their names were Michelle and Alison. And they were both teenagers and they had long golden hair. They lived in Ireland that was very pleasant. A big dragon came along and gobbled them up. They wrote a note inside the dragon to their mother that said 'we will not be home because we are inside a dragon. We are not dead but we are a little squashed from what happened to us yesterday. We are very sorry, love Alison and Michelle.' They went to sleep and posted the letter through the dragon's bottom. The end.
>
> (Field note)

The following day Sue talked about the Northern Irish dispute and asked if any of the children had relatives serving in Northern Ireland (the school has an intake of children from a local army station). The issue was discussed, as was the role of the armed forces as peacekeepers.

During the third day of that week a group of traditional Irish dancers were invited to perform to the school:

> The ladies are doing Irish dancing and we try to copy it. It was like skipping but it was on the spot and you had to lift your legs up high. I liked the way their costumes flew up. It was interesting the way they taught us and the way they had to wear soft shoes and hard ones for different dances. Last time they came I went into the middle of the circle and did some of that dancing. I can do some of the Irish dancing because my nan comes from Ireland and she taught me some of them.
>
> (Maria, Year 2)

At the end of the performance the whole school trooped out to the car park and together with the invited dancers they demonstrated some of their newly learnt jigging skills. All the school were involved including all the parents and visitors. The atmosphere was very jolly.

On the last day of the week the school gathered together in the hall to see a drama about the 1860s Irish famine. The teachers composed the play and they improvised the dialogue as they played particular characters. The atmosphere was very serious and during the performance some of the children were drawn into the drama as it unfolded:

> The Irish famine play was exciting because we didn't know who was going to be chosen to take part in the play. I was chosen. I had to be one of those children that died. That was a sad part. It was a bit scary being asked to dance around in front of the whole school but I don't mind being scared a little. You just do it. We are all children and if you make a mistake it doesn't matter.
>
> (Laura, Year 2)

The children were immersed in the drama but at the same time they were conscious of their engagement with the learning process.

> I learnt from this story that you have got to share. The rich people were not giving the poor people enough land to grow their food and in the end the potatoes went bad and they starved. There was so much sadness going round and I couldn't understand why some people were so cruel making the people get worse and worse until they died.
>
> (Laura, Year 2)

Network learning ensures that learners experience a variety of perspectives and interpretations of a particular knowledge focus. Owing to the embracing nature of the Coombes pedagogy, learners are inducted into an integrated learning experience that assists them in becoming aware of knowledge as a web of interrelations.

Conclusion

As a 'national timetable' becomes more uniform across the country, so does the time allocated to specific subjects. However, the organisation of the curriculum at Coombes differs considerably from most other Early Years schools. First, there are significant differences in terms of the active movement of children and the number of teachers who teach them during the week. Secondly, they operate a 'weak' system of ability-related curriculum groups, a few children from the top and bottom of each age range moving between cohorts. Thirdly, they maintain whole-school themes that run for as long as a term and through which the timetabled subjects are filtered. Fourthly, they have an extensive series of inspiring and exciting events that are used as a resource for the curriculum.

Coombes school is hard at work within its 'integrated code', but not wholly determined by it, nor is it ideologically blind to changing circumstances. It appropriates and incorporates reform initiatives whilst maintaining not so much a 'child-centred' approach but more of a 'child-considerate' one, in which learners are exposed to a rich diet of teaching and learning engagements judged appropriate to children of this age. Through their integrated code, learners experience knowledge as an integrated web.

The effectiveness of this approach is not only evident in the school's successful SATs results and Ofsted inspection. It can also be gleaned from the way in which children respond to their creative teaching. We consider this in the following chapter.

Chapter 5

The learning experience

Pupils have excellent attitudes to learning . . . Pupils are keen to take ownership of their own learning.

(Ofsted, 1997, para. 2, p. 1)

Learning at Coombes derives from social constructivist principles (Vygotsky, 1978). The learner does not just take in knowledge, but interprets, shapes and reconstructs the experience in a social context. Three themes identified by Pollard (1999) are particularly applicable to the experience of learning at Coombes.

First there is an emphasis on understanding learning in developmental terms. As we have seen, the school believes strongly in a spiral curriculum that enables children to revisit areas of knowledge in order to develop understanding incrementally. Returning to experiences of learning also inspires interest and confidence as children build on the knowledge they developed previously. We have also seen how the school takes into account the physically active nature of young children.

Second, a social constructivist approach draws attention to the social origins of mental functioning, emphasising the ways in which intellectual capacity is intimately connected to social activity. 'Vygotsky analysed how ways of thinking are modelled in social relations and activities, before becoming internalised and available for more independent thought' (ibid., p. 6). Learning at Coombes is a highly social activity as can be seen from the almost daily events in which either the whole school or the whole class takes part. Classroom sessions are always begun as a social activity, often continue in the same manner and, if individualised or group activities are introduced, then the climax of the session is organised as a social engagement to consider the learning objectives and processes.

The third core theme concerns how particular learning practices become established. Pollard identifies how 'communities of practice' (Lave and Wenger, 1991)

> develop in everyday social relationships in which particular ways are embedded. New learners engage in 'legitimate, peripheral participation' before they become enculturated and knowledgeable within the social practices.
>
> (Pollard, 1999, p. 7)

Coombes' learning practices are communal ones in the way that teachers and children support each other, and parents and visitors are drawn into the learning process. A school is, according to Bruner (1996), 'the place where a society shares existing knowledge and negotiates new forms' (Pollard, 1999, p. 7). It is the place where educational institutions 'do the culture's serious business' (Bruner, 1996, p. 30).

In this chapter, we focus on the ways in which Coombes employs social-constructivist principles through establishing authenticity, supporting learners' transformation of knowledge and encouraging cooperative learning.

Establishing authenticity

> The main strength of the teaching is the use of real world experiences and the quality of resources used to stimulate enthusiasm amongst pupils.
>
> (Ofsted, 1997, para. 3, p. 1)

> One thing we do is to put children into contact with reality. I think a lot of educational institutions are plastic, they are not authentic, they are not real world, and what we are aiming for here is to set children's learning in real life. Hopefully what they are getting here is equipping them for the future. The key element of it is how they actually relate to each other and to adults. If, as adults, you haven't got social skills and social intelligence, then you are going to have a heck of a difficult time. We are interested in equipping kids to live life to the full in the future and the present.
>
> (Sue Rowe)

The Coombes approach also encourages children to develop and own their own knowledge. Learning at Coombes is not a matter of learning just for the sake of educational tests or for pleasing teachers and parents (Holt, 1964). Children are encouraged to reconstruct new knowledge and processes to make them meaningful in the children's own terms:

> You have to work at your own level, and you've got to be constantly open to the children's ideas, because education only becomes genuine when they put in a very strong input. If they don't, it somehow never sits within them as a part of them-selves; they have to make that movement towards it all the time. Otherwise it's being layered on them superficially.
>
> (Sue Rowe)

In seeking to promote real learning, Coombes' teachers focus, in particular, on active learning and encouraging positive feelings.

Active learning

Play and active learning have been acknowledged as crucial to the cognitive and other developmental processes of children:

> That the child learns through making his or her own physical and mental connections with the world, through sensory explorations, personal effort, social experiences and the active seeking of meanings from experiences, has been established in the theories of psychologists and educationalists such as Froebel, Montessori, Issacs, Steiner, Vygotsky, and later, Piaget and Bruner.
>
> (Moyles, 1997, p. 9)

Coombes promotes these principles through

> hands-on, real experiences. That's why we keep sheep, and why we use the grounds so that they can actually get out there and do these things, not just look at pictures in a book or read about them or be told about them. They see the sheep being washed and sheared, they see the lambs being born, they go out and do pond dipping. They don't have to make a day's excursion to the nearest nature reserve to do that, it's part of the

ongoing curriculum and through that the children get a broad outlook on life. They know how to express themselves, and how to communicate with other people and with the environment.

(Carole)

In the 'ten in a bed' maths activity, ten children lie down next to one another, on a carpet, and a giant dice is rolled. The number showing indicates the number of children who have to roll out of the bed. 'I liked doing the rolling. We counted backwards all the way to nought. It was interesting because we rolled over and it was fun'.

(Field note, see Plate 5)

The active approach makes learning meaningful:

I made a wish for a bunk bed to come early and it came true. I liked chopping up the dates because I got to eat the prunes and to use the pips to grow a plum tree.

(Matthew, Year 1)

Being mobile and active enhanced engagement:

We are learning about life and electricity at the moment. Our teacher has wires, which we can use to make lights. We can make a fan spin around. We need two wires and a battery holder and a battery to go in it. And then you clip the wires on to the battery-holder clips. And then you join the light clips up to the wire to make the light work or the fan work. We enjoy it because of the way that we are doing it. We don't sit down all the time.

(David, Year 2)

The learners literally 'beat the bounds' of the school:

The children all took a stick and walked all around the boundary of the school grounds. At various places they beat the fences and sang a song. They dabbled in a pond, splashed the water, beat the trees and conjured images and stories on the walk. 'We were beating the boundary. It was fun, really really fun.' The learning objectives incorporated map making, the use of compass points and the history of the 'parish'.

(Field note)

Theresa (parent) had benefited from the school's 'open-door' policy, going to the school two or three times to have a 'really good look round'. She was impressed with the children's application:

> The children were all busy. All the time they were occupied, there was no misbehaving. There seemed to be adults with them on each table. Other schools were sitting one teacher to thirty plus children. And my child's very active. I just knew that if he went to a school where he had to sit his bottom on that chair and copy what was on the board or wait for the teacher's attention, his mind would be gone. So he's come here, and he's just flourished.

The body is the prime symbol of the self and the prime determinant of the self (Sparkes, 1999), and young children experiment with their bodies and express themselves through their bodies.

> During the more 'active engagements' there were lots of shared smiles and laughter. They played with expressions as they laughed at themselves and the situation; expressed amazement; made facial and verbal connections with someone else; screwed up their faces with contorted smiles as they experienced strange noises like the bagpipes and tactile encounters while making porridge. However, they did not overdo the excitement, they acted calmly with interest.
>
> (Field note)

Combining active learning and the replication of practices can heighten authenticity and bring a sense of individuality:

> I painted the ceiling in the classroom like Michelangelo did. It was interesting because I don't usually paint ceilings. It was exciting because I was doing something different to the other children.
>
> (Alison, Year 2)

Active learning engages the senses:

> It is interesting being with the sheep because you can feel the warm wool and texture, and it is soft like my hair. It is

interesting feeling things. It feels lovely when you get your hands in the mixing bowl when we do cooking.

(Michelle, Year 2)

Any opportunity to include a sense of taste was always included in any investigation. 'When we did our Spanish topic we made paella. It had octopus and mussels. It was tasty and interesting making it because we don't usually eat these things' (Gigi, Year 2).

Active learning involves role play, particularly appropriate for young children who use narrative as an organising tool (Fox, 1989). Rachel had been discussing the paintings of Mary Cassatt with her class, which portrayed tender moments between mothers and daughters, but looking at the paintings was not enough. She arranged for the class to observe a mother bathing her baby, with the children gathered round in a circle:

> We feel that it's really important to give them a really exciting stimulus so they can actually see a tender moment, see the mother looking lovingly at the child, helping wash the child, brushing her daughter's hair or washing the child's toes or the child just sitting with her mother as she's sewing.

> The children would then do a 'writers' workshop', some encouraging others, some sitting quietly and reflecting, the teacher also supporting, trying to get them to feel themselves as writers, believing in themselves and building up their confidence. Once that has taken hold, you can start to correct their work in a constructive way – but not until.

(Sue Humphries)

Similarly, being a designer encourages learners to reconstruct knowledge into their own representations:

> We did our own designs on a piece of paper. They were photocopied at lunchtime to make lots of copies. In the afternoon we stuck them on to a piece of paper how we wanted them. This is the design I chose. I have repeated it. We need to do each section the same colour to make it look like a design. If I did them all different colours it would not look much like a design. It is all the leaves and flowers on a theme. We brought these things in from outside. There is a fir cone, this is a catkin. I often see

this sort of design being done on a computer. You can see designs on walls, cushions, bedclothes, wrapping paper, jars, and clothes.

Authentic learning contexts allow learners the opportunity to transform learning into a problem-solving experience, 'I look forward to doing experiments like the lights and batteries. It is like testing things. I don't care if it goes wrong. If I was a witch and I had to make a new potion in my cauldron I would experiment' (Craig, Year 2).

This kind of role play is empowering:

> It's having that curiosity of mind and of spirit, of wanting to know because it's interesting for itself. It's realising that you, too, can do it; you, too, can be a scientist, a true researcher.
>
> (Sue Rowe)

It increases the fun of learning:

> Amy was pretending to be a baby for Miss Rowe when we were talking about bones and growing. I like it when Miss Rowe encourages us to pretend. She does things interestingly with her voice as she plays a part. We did a play of the three pigs. We had a really bad wolf and we all joined in. It was fun.
>
> (Michelle, Year 2)

Role play increases learning effectiveness (Jeffrey, 2003):

> It was very very very sad when the teachers were pretending to cry about their dead children who had died from starvation in Ireland. I really didn't like it when people started dying. It was like it was really happening.
>
> (Laura, Year 2)

It allows experimentation with one's self and an opportunity to see things from other perspectives, a critical feature in being creative:

> In the RE lesson we had to play a part and then think about that person's life. You get a chance to be somebody else. Statues are interesting because you are stuck like that. It is enjoyable

because we are being things we don't normally do. It was good pretending to be angry.

(Simon, Year 1; see Plate 6)

Judy used a 'Roamer', a mobile robot operated by remote control to increase active engagement:

The children devised their own routes, laying down carpet tiles, walking along the routes themselves and turning in right angles, 90 degree turns. This has carried over into PE sessions and music sessions where they've been singing and dancing, doing movements as robots, and actually making these turns.

Technical manipulation is appreciated by children:

Some computer programmes are enjoyable because you can make things on them and play around with it. You get control of it because the computer can't do it all its own. You are controlling it like you would control a robot.

(Michelle, Year 2)

Generating positive feelings

Feeling positively about learning combines the emotions and the cognitive in an experience that draws the learner inside the activity.

The children are copying Miss Daniel's stick rhythms. They are wondering what is going to happen next, thinking that this is fun. It is fun because you have to learn to copy, think about it and then do it. That's the tricky part. Altogether it is like a game but it's fun. They are looking happy because it's fun. They are not misbehaving because they don't want to miss out on the fun. You get to hear the different music and you have to learn it.

(Laura, Year 2)

It is of great importance to Coombes' teachers how children feel about their learning. Feelings hold the key to cognition. So there is much talk of excitement, joy, fun, happiness, confidence. Everything they do is fun. Sue Rowe recalls her first inspirational memory, digging a hole, and the children wanting to get in the hole because it was so exciting, to see what was underneath their feet and finding the joy in quite ordinary things, things that you always take for granted, you can never consider. And it was seeing children falling on to the ground with excitement at seeing an earthworm coming out and it was using that hole so the children were actually collecting clay. And I remember we were making small waterproof bowls from the clay, and giving children some water to carry across the playground. The joy and excitement that something as simple as that generated for me was marvellous – the real stuff of life and of education.

Keith's 6-year-old son was sent to the school because 'all the children are happy, and the school develops the child. He has become aware of himself and is a very inquisitive child, as are most of the children'. He contrasts it with his own experiences of school,

I hated it, and they were undoubtedly the worst years of my life. When it came to discussing school for my child, I had to be persuaded to come here, but when I actually came I found it was wonderful. I walked past the windows and saw all these happy faces, and quite frankly I have to eat my words, because he's had a marvellous time here, and it's developed him very well.

Keith was looking ahead:

I believe the children should have fun. They should learn to be able to develop themselves. When it comes for them to go out in the wide world in the twenty-first century it's going to be exceedingly difficult for them to find jobs and careers and I think they may well have to experience the turmoil of having to retrain two or three times within their working lives. The school is preparing them well for the ability to adjust and to develop themselves rather than having something thrust at them.

This makes a good basis for learning things like the core subjects. Their success at that

comes from the happiness that emanates from the school. All the children are willing to learn. They're so busy they're happy to learn, they don't even know they're learning half the time. Two or three years on now, he's Year 2 and his reading and writing have absolutely blossomed in the last couple of months. Meanwhile he's had this happy experience of school which he'll take with him throughout life.

'Fun' and 'happiness' does not mean a free-for-all. Children's natural and copious resources have to be channelled to some extent. Theresa, for example, was concerned to channel her child's confidence 'in the right direction'. In some respects, he was 'over-confident' and he had found it hard in the nursery school having to 'knuckle under at times. But at the end of his first day in infant school his teacher asked me to come and see her, and the first thing she said was "This child is so gorgeous I cannot wait to have him in my classroom"'. Theresa 'sort of preened' and thought 'Wonderful! I just hope it lasts for ever!' Martin's daughter had 'been here six months, she's as happy as we could ever have hoped for, and on the back of that she's learning more than we could ever have imagined'. Gina's daughter 'talks about it the whole time. Her love of books is amazing. They nurture a love of books right from the word go'.

Sue Humphries is sure

> It really has something to do with a confident personality. If the setting is right it's going to help you to fulfil yourself as a person. So that all those qualities that make you fun to be with are burnished. They're going to be brought to the fore and emphasised. You might be a clever barrister, or a brilliant author or painter or road-sweeper or waitress but it's going to be the personal qualities that you bring to the job and the way that you relate to other people that's going to mean that you're happy in your life and filled with a sense of achievement and purpose. Education can foster those qualities, and education goes on and on.

Dee's daughter was 'a very bright and receptive child, but she was crippled by her lack of confidence'. She might easily have 'become very intimidated at a very early age' in the current pressurised National Curriculum environment. But at Coombes, 'everything is just fostered and encouraged. Because there is no regimentation, the children find it very easy to find their own level and just pick everything up. Some don't get left miles behind because of an attitude difference'. Celebrating achievement enhances feelings of well-being:

> It was good because Mrs Daniels was proud of me. It made me happy because I like standing up in front of the music teacher. I like standing up and people saying 'Well done!' I like being asked to come and stand up in front of the group because I have done something good.

Children themselves are aware of the importance of celebrating achievement for the development of confidence

> Owen is standing on the table with some writing in his hand. The teachers could be saying 'Well done, Owen', and giving him a clap because he has done the star piece of work. Owen would be thinking 'Wow! I have made the teachers very pleased'. He likes standing on the table because we were not allowed to do it normally. It is a treat. He feels happy and confident. This will help him with his writing because it will make him listen more and will give him more confidence. I've never really felt like that.
>
> (Laura, Year 2)

This confidence, once established, seems to stay with them. James, a parent, felt

> They are confident in the world as they go out today as 6 or even 5-year-olds. They're holding an adult conversation and you are happy for them because they're talking sense. You're not embarrassed by your children. If they've been to Coombes, they really are different. They're always constantly surprising you.

With confidence comes the competence to be critical, rather than simply desiring to please the teacher. Lynn (parent) felt

> Life is just such an experience to them, they just don't accept anything, they question every single thing. It's like if you tell a child something, they're going to test it out. If they prove it for themselves they learn it.

The generation of positive feelings is encouraged by the development of an 'adventure culture' of learning through providing opportunities to experiment, play, be innovative and exercise control.

A constant stream of novel encounters maintains the adventure culture:

> There are surprises on the computer painting. If you have scribbled on the computer you can still find things by looking through the painting. You can make a mess and still find something real in it.
>
> (Alice, Year 1)

'It is exciting when you haven't seen things before, when it is new, like the sheep being treated for foot rot by the vet' (Sally, Year 1). Uncertainty is intriguing: 'It would be exciting for me to play on the computer because you don't know what's going to come up on the screen (Alice, Year 1).

Open-ended possibilities are important for stimulating anticipation and excitement:

> We had to collect together twigs and leaves and make a nest and then we drew them. It was interesting because you could use the clay as well. It was exciting because nobody knew what they were going to do. They had to decide what they were going to use. We could choose what we used. We didn't know what it would look like before we started.
>
> (Maria, Year 1)

The teachers have created challenges taking into account children's fears and desires for risk-taking. Risk-taking is part of learning: 'I had to read to the whole of class. It was a bit scary but I felt happy at the end of doing it' (Ricky, Year 1). Learning about light and darkness becomes fun for the children and they experiment with 'search and recover' strategies. Anticipation is an emotion that draws on past experiences of risk-taking and challenge, 'When we go in the dark house it is dark and we can't see. We have to find some toys. We have a torch. It was fun because you keep on bumping into people (Hannah, Nursery). As Sue Humphries puts it:

As you grow, you are making up your own story inside yourself and that story has to be filled with happiness – it will be filled with unhappiness quite naturally – but its construct, together with the intellectual abilities that are being developed has to be happy, glad, anticipatory, so that you come to school filled with curiosity and a sense of 'I want to be here and I want to join in'.

Transforming knowledge

Learners interpret knowledge according to their experience and interests and express it in their own terms. They thus 'impose order on chaos' (Reggio Emilia, 1996). McGuiness (1999, p. 1) notes that

> Developing thinking skills is supported by theories of cognition which see learners as active creators of their knowledge and frameworks of interpretation. Learning is about searching out meaning and imposing structure.

Young children generate meaning by filtering and then transforming knowledge through their imaginations. Children experiment with imaginative constructions and play with ideas (Craft, 2002). In a maths lesson, a group of Year 2 children are given the task of identifying specific shapes and explaining their properties. They construct different shapes from construction equipment, then give them a meaning by filtering them through their imagination and personal life connections:

> One child says, 'You can make a diamond, a big one.' Another says, 'I'm a builder, I need another big one like this.' 'Look at my eyeballs like triangles.' 'Look at my hat.' 'I've made a clucking hen.' 'I can make a salamander, I invented him.' 'I have made a shammon [TV character].' The teacher says, 'I can see Robin through his Connect cube.' The child says quietly, 'I can see your face.' 'This is a telescope.' A child put his head into a 3D cube and says he has made a soldier's helmet.
>
> (Field note)

Narrative is a common mode of children using their imaginations to transform knowledge. This is, in fact, their main form of cognitive activity (Fox, 1989). While drawing a map of the school grounds, after 'beating the bounds' of the school, a group of children construct their own story of an event on the map:

'Go that way and then that way and then back into the den and hide the treasure underneath. That's why it says 100. Ping Ping Ping Ping.' 'Out crawled the captain. There is lots of wool. There's a squirrel. Oh no, that's Captain Hook.' 'If that is Captain Hook, then who is that man?' 'It's the enemy. Where is Mr Smith?' 'He's got a gun he must be the blaster.' 'He looks a hundred.' 'Look, axes guns and knives.' 'Look he's picking his nose.' 'In this bit there were lots of pirates climbing up there.' 'I swung one and knocked that one down.' 'There is Captain Hook, look.' 'Where?' 'And there's me. I'm driving a car and then going to run over that bear's claw.' 'Look, the goblin is there.' 'Mister Speed is being knocked over.' 'Pretend I was a dog and you heard a noise outside and you went to investigate.'
(Field note)

Children are given time and support to enable them to filter learning experiences through their preferred media. Curriculum objectives are then realised by encouraging the learners to show their knowledge through a narrative.

We went beating the boundaries to remind us not to go outside them or we might be run over by a car. It happened in the olden days when the children were beaten to remind them not to leave the village boundaries. Beating them meant they would remember. Some of them died because they were whacked so hard. They had to stay in their part of the area. If you lived outside the area you would not be given any help.

The reproduction of this historical knowledge is found to be much easier for the children when using narrative than when being tested about the facts of the situation. When asked by the researcher, 'What have you learnt this morning?' the children's responses were very limited, but when asked to 'Tell me the story of beating the bounds', they gave much richer answers.

This filtering of knowledge through the young learners' imagination manifests itself in talking:

'Children solve practical tasks with the help of their speech, as well as with their eyes and hands. This unity of perception, speech and actions which ultimately produces internalization of the visual field, constitutes the central subject matter for any analysis of the origin of uniquely human forms of behaviour' (Mind in Society, p. 26). Language is (in Vygotsky's sense as in Dewey's) a way of sorting out one's thoughts about things.

(Bruner, 1986, p. 72)

A boy arrives to collect his Tudor house from the street plan laid out in the hall but finds it is missing. His reaction is not despair but imaginative reflection as he uses the models of houses on the street to construct a story:

> He wanders around saying, 'It smells like a chocolate, it is brown. I am staying to keep an eye out for it.' He marches around the paths. 'It couldn't have moved because it has no legs. Perhaps it has fallen into the sea. Perhaps someone else has taken it by mistake. We'll act like sniffer dogs. Maybe a magician has disappeared it.'

(Field note)

Learning experiences are made meaningful by active learning twinned with imaginative transformations:

> I felt the vibrations by touching the harp while he played it. I liked the music. I imagined that I was in a field riding a horse. I then jumped off the horse into space. I jumped on to a planet and then I jumped on to a star. I then went into a spaceship and there was nothing in it. It was the world and I was falling down on to it, back on to my horse.

Encouraging imaginative responses was a strategy used by the teachers to enhance learning, for example by encouraging children to make up number stories:

> There were two monkeys up a tree and the ground began to shake and two more monkeys climbed up the tree to join them.
> There were three flowers and a horse ate one of them.
> There were four flowers and a pig ate two of them and a girl came along and picked one.
> There were four ducks and eight flew down to join them.
> There were three trees and one was chopped down.
> They were five birds and a crocodile ate one.

They were two flowers and two more grew and pig came along and ate one.
The little girl saw five fairies but one was so scared it had to go back to fairyland.

(Reception children, field note)

Similarly, when Sue asked the children to imagine what it would be like if their muscles grew faster than their bones and vice versa, the children used their imaginations to develop their knowledge of the body:

I'd be all floppy if my bones didn't grow.
My skin would be hanging down off the end of my fingers.
My nose would be dangling down there.
My earrings will be down touching the floor.
If my bones grew when my body didn't, I would be all skinny.
I would have extra lumps all over me.
My bones would be stretching my body so I would be very thin.
I'd be like a skinny soldier and bones would be sticking out of my skin.
My brain would be getting squashed.

The extensive focus on language development and discussion enables children to develop a disposition for analysing learning experiences metaphorically:

I felt the harp vibrating and I listened to the music. When I felt the vibrations it made me think of a nail pricking my finger very gently.

We all went into the hall and heard Keith play the harp. It sounded like the sea swishing and swoshing. I have been to Paignton on holiday and I played in the sea. It was charming.

Taking ownership of knowledge through the imagination is to make it meaningful in terms of the self. The knowledge then becomes valuable to the learner as an expression of the self and any encouragement of this process is extending the worth of the particular knowledge the teacher is exploring. Knowledge augments the extensions of self (Reggio Emilia, 1996).

Learning cooperatively

Ownership of knowledge and control over learning is also gained in interactive social contexts. Participation among and between teachers, pupils, parents and others is a big feature of the learning experience at Coombes. Everyone who passes through the doors at Coombes is included in the pedagogic experience (see also Chapters 1 and 6).

Children reinterpret, in their own terms, the teachers' articulations:

> When Sue and Carol started a discussion about boys having babies one Year 1 boy affirmed the suggestion by telling them that 'I like babies'. Learners offer their own contributions to the learning contexts, whether heard or not. One of the teachers says, 'All the pots from all the children are in the kiln'. A Year 1 child says, 'except for the juniors'. A reception child adds to the teacher's instructions about planting daffodils, by exemplifying the instructions to the whole class, 'not upside down like this'.
>
> (Field note)

Celebrating innovative suggestions from learners helps create a co-participative climate for learning,

> Jude asks the Year 2 group how many they need to get from 75 to 100. She then commends a girl who offers a solution as to how to make the calculation: add on or take off the five and count in tens and then remember the five.
>
> (Field note)

In this creative climate, learners feel free to make suggestions to improve the quality of lessons:

> Miss Rowe said we were going to collect some greenery for an Irish display and I went up to Miss Rowe and said, 'Shall I sit on top of a chair on the table?' And then the class went outside and got lots of green leaves and they settled it around me and Betty put some on my head, which drooped down and gave me eye ache. It was a really good Green Museum, and I was a real model. They put leaves and branches up over my shoulders. The children concentrated because they wanted it to look artistic.
>
> (Rachael, Year 2; see Plate 7)

Co-participation (Reggio Emilia, 1996) brings learners into the learning process as contributors:

> A Year 1 girl in Carol's class reminds all the children that the task they are being asked to do – wax relief – has been done before and she points to an example on the wall. This is not seen as a criticism on her part, but a contribution to remind others that they have previous experience of the practice.
>
> (Field note)

Co-participation spreads to peer participation:

> Sophie (Year 2) asks another child if she can use her hands to help with doubling numbers and the pair of them use this strategy to complete the task.
>
> (Field note)

> Some new reception children have arrived in Judy's class and she asks the indigenous group to dramatise one of their favourite stories. So an audience is created and the children improvise the characters' behaviours imaginatively from the story as it is read.
>
> (Field note)

Another form of co-participation valued at Coombes is that of reversing teacher and learner roles. Children often take visitors on guided tours of the school. In some cases they take over teaching roles, as when three Year 2 children were instructed to assist the researcher in the art of making a 'smudged picture' with pastels:

> 'Then you get a white for the sky and rub it on. Do it dead gently and smudge it in.' 'With your fingers like Miss Davis taught us.' 'It makes a good effect, it makes it a better picture.' 'You can smudge the tops of the mountains but don't do bumps.' 'You get some blue for the sky and leave some gaps of white to make it look like winter.' 'You also leave a gap for the sun. You have to make it look really really misty.' 'You can use pink and purple and brown near the sun.' 'It has to be nearly dark to make it seem misty. This is going to be really great.' 'You can do what you like but it has to look like a dark sun.' 'Do it very lightly. Leave a space for the sun. Use pinks and

oranges and yellows.' 'You have to use all these colours because the sky changes when it gets dark. You have to use pinks and oranges and yellows.' 'Don't use any more blue, but put some pink in there.' 'Then there's the hard bit where you have to put really dotty lines across it.' 'Now leave it. That's good, that. Now you need to get the black and do little dotted lines where you have smudged the colours in.'

(Field note)

Taking on a teaching role gives children a measure of control and an opportunity to be creative. In this case the children mix their teacher's expressions with their experience to describe the process of smudge painting. In doing so they are also developing their understanding of the teaching and learning process.

The contributions are not only between teacher and learner. There are dialogues that develop between learners:

Sue asks her mixed 5–7-year-old children how they would fill up an alien's empty brain and the children not only use their imagination but they confront each other's contributions.
'I would do it in a laboratory.'
'I would do it by telling.'
'You can't. Because it hasn't got anything in its brain to think with.'
'He wouldn't be able to remember anything.'
'You could make him go to sleep and then open his head a little to put the right information on his brain.'

The process of discussion opens up avenues for learning which include philosophical debates:

During the discussion with Sue about how babies learn, the following question came out of the blue and was taken on by the others. 'This question is a hard one because how did the first person in the world know all the things about the world?' 'God taught them.' 'But he was a little baby.' 'How did the world get made?' 'How did the first person get made?' 'How did the whole universe gets made?' 'How did life grow?' There followed lots of chatter permeated with questions and assertions and answers.

(Field note)

In pursuance of co-participation, some discussions of the learning process are included in the pedagogic process:

> Sue asks her class how they learn. The answers not only contribute to knowledge but the contributory climate encourages them to share their knowledge. 'I listen and you teach us.' 'You need to use your ears to listen, your nose to smell and your eyes to see.' 'You need to listen most of the time and to be quiet.' 'It is like you have dots in your brain and they are all joined up.' 'You think about it and stuff like that as well.' 'Your brain is telling you how to use your eyes.' 'The college tells you what to tell us and you tell us and we get the answer.'
>
> (Field note)

Creative co-participation in teaching and learning involving the whole community was exemplified by the annual Fire of London topic. The children were told the story and a form of 'common knowledge' (Edwards and Mercer, 1987) with teachers and peers was developed as they retold it verbally and in writing:

> The houses were too close and so the fire spread quickly. They had to run away quickly down to the river and get away by boat. The wind was blowing quickly and it was too strong to get across the river. When they caught a fish they didn't need to cook them because they were all boiled by the warm water of the London fire. Nine people died. One man told them to pull down the places where they stored things and the fire couldn't go any further:
>
> (Susan, Year 1)

Families were then invited in to be co-participants by asking them to assist their children in constructing a model of a Tudor building at home with their children:

> As a child I could not remember any of the events, but because I became involved with my children I learnt a lot more about it. It involved the parents quite a lot because they work together with the children to make the houses. It is not obligatory but during the process of making the house the children have learnt a great deal about that period of time in history. They have learnt about all the different perspectives and what was it like to be a child in that time. Not just the straight historical facts.

You learn all sorts of things, not just history. It is to do with making things, technology, fire safety, simultaneously taught through one really clever well-thought-out project. It draws out all the strengths of each age group within the class as well as home life. We went to the library to find out what the houses looked like and how to put things together. Then when the great day comes it is really exciting. Houses start trickling in during the course of the week and they are all assembled in the hall. It becomes more and more interesting and absorbing each day as new houses arrive.

(Parent governor)

The children cooperated with their parents and with peers in the construction of some of the buildings in the classroom.

We put one box on top of another. We stuck paper all over it and then painted it. My dad cut all the little sticks to put on it and then we did the black bits and then we did the doors and windows.

(Tony, Year 1)

All the metre-high houses, churches and warehouses were installed in the hall on a street plan. This was then used for a week as a resource for maths work in mapping, direction, measurement, shape recognition and tessellation. The children used the 'roads' frequently, often on their own to traverse the hall to other parts of the building. Then on Thursday afternoon all the children gathered up their houses and, along with parents, grandparents and friends, the whole school troops out to the field and lays out the houses on the street map for the last time:

We set fire to them. We smile at how much time we spent on them and then we burn them. For one of my children it became a real problem. She just did not want to burn it after she had made it. At the very last moment she decided not to let it be burnt and it still lies in the loft at home. But both of them can remember the key facts, what the buildings were made of, which is why they burnt so quickly, the date and how to make things. We make history come alive through the buildings. It is never boring and this is the third time we have done it. It is never dull.

(Parent governor)

Plate 1 Cooking together

Plate 2 Celebrating an annual event

Plate 3　Investigating forces

Plate 4 Literacy in the environment

Plate 5 Reality maths

Plate 6 Role-playing religious education

Plate 7 Co-participation

Plate 8 Reality history

The children are forced into weighing up a difficult decision of ownership, 'I don't really want mine to be burnt but I will let it be burnt. However, I won't mind if it doesn't actually catch fire'.

While taking care to observe safety regulations, the headteacher then sets light to the 'baker's shop' and the children, staff and parents collectively engage in a learning experience never to be forgotten (Plate 8). The vividness of the children's descriptions exemplify their excitement:

> The houses are alight 'The one next to me is on fire.' 'Wow, look at them fly into the sky. They're gliding.' 'Bye Bye. Some people have escaped by flying. They're witches.' There are smiles, cheers and loud laughs as one collapses. 'My one is burnt to bits. There is no more life.' There are loud 'Oohs!' as one of the last houses eventually succumbs. There are no complaints about the cold bitter wind. There is a loud 'whoo' as the wind suddenly blows the ash towards the children. The church is the last to go. After the burning the children and parents disperse, some back to the classroom, others to buy hot dogs for sale in the car park.
>
> (Field note)

Some grandparents saw the learning experience as unique and extremely relevant:

> This is fantastic, isn't it? It is so realistic, isn't it? It's much better compared with what we had when we were at school. We investigated the history of each of the houses. Last year, when the fire had expired there was just one house left. I don't know how they did it. It was quite an intriguing sight. We made the house together. They get quite involved in doing it.
>
> School was more boring when we were at school. They don't forget it when they do something like this. To see a re-enactment of this, Pudding Lane and the whole fire is wonderful. It clings to the children, much more than 20,000 words in a book. I'd forgotten all about it but this brings it all back.

The parent governor regarded this as a

> key event which constitutes the magic of Coombes. Everything comes together, they have all got a common objective. There are

various events during the year which may be different in style and content which appeal to different children at their stage of development and spark off something in them which is what teachers are after.

Conclusion

Coombes creates an authentic learning experience that recognises children's active dynamism and combines it with an openness to the way learners make experiences meaningful. Longitudinal research into the effects of the 1990s reforms carried out in primary schools found that pedagogies that minimised consideration of the learners' capacities and interests and the involvement of the learner in the objectives and the processes of teaching and learning resulted in 'a sense of children in flight from an experience of learning that they found unsatisfying, unmotivating and uncomfortable' (Pollard *et al.*, 2000, p. 103). Teaching and learning programmes that do not strive for authenticity and support learner's control and ownership of knowledge may well result in disengaged learning (ibid.).

Children start off being creative (Beetlestone, 1998), prefer some control over their learning and welcome opportunities to fantasise and to use their imagination (Pollard, 1999). Children are equipped with the capacities and perceptive tools for organising and reacting to senses, for seeking exchange – embodying the actions of the semiologist and detective – to hypothesise, to deal with missing explanations and to reconstruct facts (Reggio Emilia, 1996). To be creative, learners often have to tear things down and build them up again by transforming them (Beetlestone, 1998). It is argued that it is not possible to teach creativity, only to set the conditions (Smith *et al.*, 1999), a task Coombes sees as essential.

These principles are reflected in Coombes teachers' views on assessment of learning. They are as keen as any others on raising achievement, but they argue that any assessment of children's learning should be broader than that envisaged in the SATs or by Ofsted's criteria:

> We are concerned to give similar consideration to those immeasurable aspects of education. Not all end results can be reproduced as a set of statistics, but they are equally vital if we are to provide children with the means to become committed life-long learners. Our fear is that education is not best serving

a substantial proportion of pupils and that in years to come there could be an increase in the numbers of disaffected young people in this country. We are committed to offering a challenging, focused, relevant and broad education, which will contain 'something for everyone' as an engaged learner.

(Rowe and Humphries, 2001, p. 161)

The National Curriculum is valued, but a high value is also placed on the ability to engage in social learning and personal development:

Education is important for learning to read and write, etc. However much more important, I think, is that people talk to each other, can reason, recognise another point of view, be tolerant, be accepting and to have respect for oneself. You get respect for yourself if you have got respect for others.

(Carol)

To support a broader assessment practice, the headteacher interviewed each Year 2 child prior to their leaving and forwarded to their next school a Coombes assessment of each child, constructed together with that child. A typical one reads:

Joe has plenty of friends and he has a wide choice of companions when he goes out to the playground. Asked about memorable days, Joe described St Patrick's Day and the pleasure he had from the Irish dancing. He was also impressed by the delivery of the stones and the making of Arthur's seat as well as the building of Coombeshenge. Joe related many early experiences in a meaningful way. 'At Easter two rabbits came and put eggs down for us to take home and eat.' He thought this was a 'great celebration plan'. As distinct curriculum entities Joe prefers science and maths and says that he 'is not so keen on music or hall times'. A long-term ambition of Joe's is to do something with sport and earn a living at it. Asked about his understanding about right and wrong he stated: 'If I accidentally trip someone over, that's not being naughty but if I do it on purpose then it's naughty!' 'I think it's all about the things you do on purpose.' Joe stressed the benefit to everyone of being kind and understanding and his view of himself is that he makes a good try at practising these virtues; this is a genuine conception of his behaviour held by his teachers. He attempts to stay on task although he finds it taxing but also feels that he is getting better with every experience. Favourite books are animal books, stories of monsters and stories with a strong line in adventure. We need to use his interests as much as possible in his continuing education.

(Sue Humphries)

Children themselves found the experience rewarding:

Being interviewed by Miss Humphreys about me was exciting and interesting because you have deep thoughts that you don't usually think about. It was exciting thinking about my future life.

(Michelle, Year 2)

The government report into creativity and culture (NACCCE, 1999) suggested that there were three tasks for creativity in education: encouraging positive identities; fostering a language for the twenty-first century that included playfulness, flexibility and innovation; and generating a habit of learning and being creative. Coombes has provided a learning model for these objectives.

Chapter 6

Coombes as a learning community

What are the factors behind the success of Coombes? We see these deriving from three main sources. First, there has been a charismatic agent at the centre of the development of the school. Coombes was not made in a day; in fact it has taken Sue Humphries a lifetime. She would be the first, however, to point, secondly, to the contributions of others and the democratic and collaborative way in which they work. Thirdly, there is the involvement of the whole community and the spirit of *communitas* that pervades the school. Coombes is a paradigm case of a learning community. The heart of its success lies in that concept.

Visionary leadership

At the centre of policy and planning there has been visionary leadership – played down by Sue Humphries herself, since she preferred to see it coming through in others, and in the life of the school. Carol Cook, a long-serving teacher at the school, was captured by Sue's charisma as early as her interview for the post she now holds:

> Sue explained to me that she wanted to put the school back into its rightful setting, because it had a most beautiful backdrop of fields and woods, but had been left by the architects as a barren site. And I thought, 'Oh, this is a woman I could work with!' and it just went from there.

When Sue retires, noted Sue Rowe, 'it will need someone to step into her shoes, with similar visions and a similar inspirational charismatic style'. Leadership may be distributed and shared, but there is still a 'critical agent' (Woods, 1995) at the centre of events acting as catalyst. The literature refers to the importance of a school's history (see, for example, Cocklin *et al.*, 1996). In the case of Coombes, this is to a large extent Sue's own life history and her personal long-term vision, which entails what Hameyer (1996) calls a 'long-distance running exercise':

> Twenty-five years ago I had a plan of sorts, a whole lot of things I wanted to realise. One of them was a community school with a team of teachers working in it who very much cared for each other as well as caring for the children. And I had a few ideas about a setting in which I hoped education would take place. But it wasn't a ten-year plan. It was a twenty-five- or thirty- or forty-year plan. So I'm not going to finish it before it's time for me to retire, because I'm not anywhere close to the realisation that I had or the dream I had at the beginning. So it was bigger than I believed it was.

At the centre of the Coombes achievement, then, is the charismatic agent, the head, who had the vision, faith, values and beliefs to launch the project, resolve and patience to sustain and develop it, and personal skills and judgement in surrounding herself with and inspiring like-minded people to contribute to the enterprise. Fullan and Hargreaves (1992) recall Tom's (1984) view of teaching as a moral business, firstly in helping to shape the generations of the future, secondly in the discretionary judgements they make in classrooms. 'Because teaching is a moral craft, it has purpose for those who do it. There are things that teachers value, that they want to achieve through their teaching' (Fullan and Hargreaves, 1992, p. 29). Too often, teachers' purposes are overlooked by reformers and they do not have a voice. At Coombes, there is a strong sense of purpose. When we asked Sue how she managed so often to get her own way with exterior bureaucratic forces, she replied, 'Well, I think having a reputation as an eccentric helps'. Part of this 'eccentricity' perhaps is Sue's ability to challenge the 'givens' of school, which Sarason (1982) feels is one of the most important factors in inducing change. Some of these 'givens' are the inside classroom as the main context of teaching and learning, the sharp division between inside and outside school, the playground as a plain hard surface, the National Curriculum, assessment. At Coombes, Sue retains her independent vision. Certain aspects of the National

Curriculum are welcome, others are an irritant, but, by and large, it is subsumed within their grand design. Sue makes capital in other ways. To run and develop such a project requires funds and services from others:

> We need money for repairs. For example, a pond cracked in last year's drought and will cost about £600 to put right. We also need money for ephemeral things, like feeding sheep, paying vets' bills, giving expenses to people like hot-air balloonists. You can't actually see what they've left you with. They are the intangibles, but they are the things that give a quality and a certain edge to this kind of education, if it's what you believe in.

It also means entrepreneurial skills, powers of persuasion and considerable determination. To get opera singers, under-belly horse riders, internationally acclaimed writers, helicopter pilots, para-chutists, etc. to the school, Sue feels, rests on 'the way you present the case, the tone of the approach, and the doggedness of the approach and, of course, the way a group decides how it spends its money'. A colleague reported that 'when a small circus visited the area, Sue was absolutely determined we were going to get this camel into the playground and she did it'. Why was it so important?

> It was to do with the Epiphany and the journey of the wise men, and it was really something that just put that special memory into all the talk that had gone on. Children are talked at by teachers for hundreds of hours, and so much of it must sail directly over them.

In many ways, Coombes is an expression of Sue's self. Woods (1990) has argued elsewhere that a teacher can both find a means of expression and give expression to a curriculum area. Despite the constraints and opposing pressures, teachers can engage with the curriculum at a deep personal level. Sue shows that this can apply to the school itself. Like many of the teachers interviewed by Nias (1989), it provides opportunities to 'be yourself,' to 'be whole' and to 'be natural'. As a major, long-term project, with many branches and operating at a number of levels, Coombes repre-sents a considerable part of a life's work. Holistic in its aims, it has been holistic in its claims on the time, energies, creativity, patience, perseverance and enthusiasm of its sponsors. This includes the staff as a whole, and the body of parents. Sue's colleagues

> aren't just in this for money. They're in it for a certain amount of personal power, and that personal power has to be released. They have to be part of the decision-making. They've got to see their personality reflected in the overall school pattern.

Creativity through team work

> The school's democratic management structure is very effective and assures the school's total commitment towards high achievement in all aspects of pupil development.
>
> (Ofsted, 1997, para. 7, p. 2)

Sue is supported by a staff of like-minded colleagues who share her vision and are equally enthusiastic. Some have written articles, books, appeared on television. While Sue provides leadership, it is leadership by example. 'There is no line manager,' she says. 'It's consensus politics here. If a teacher can see a fun way to deal with something, then they know they can go and do it'. There is no bland conformity among them. 'All our staff have got very different ideas about what should be done,' said Sue. 'They don't always concur'. Consequently the group is very creative. Sue Humphries believed

> There's no greater educator really than the influence of the group. Every group feels its way towards what's right for that group. I think sometimes very strong leadership can stop a group feeling its way outward and onward. For me, the entire movement outwards has got to be wholly felt within the group. It mustn't favour some people and not others, and I think there can be some odd distinctions about who has the best ideas. You don't have the best ideas because you're the head, or because you've been here longer than anybody else.

Teachers thus work as a team in which they are all leaders. Sue reported:

> Everybody has an inner light, and it's giving space and opportunities for that to be brought out, whether at staff meetings . . . You can sometimes think 'Oh, that's a whacky idea'. Then

when you examine it, you find out that there is something really very trenchant in that way of thinking. It's a matter of accepting the ideas, sometimes sitting for a moment or two in silence. Our staff meetings tend to be rather long drawn out and rather hesitant sometimes, but that's because everybody's stopping and thinking and looking at what other people have submitted. The ideas, as they are produced, direct everybody's thinking, and the one that does that is naturally the leader for that moment and probably for that activity.

If you're working in a very comradely way, other people's interests will work on you. If somebody says, 'I really think we should do *The Water Babies*', everybody's digesting this idea and thinking, 'Yes, but how?' She'll then go on and say, 'I see one of us as Tom, and here we all are, and there's the children doing the different features of the book', and breathing life into it and taking up the moral issues out of it. So you find yourself caught up in *The Water Babies* out of one person's enthusiasm for it. If you're susceptible to each other you want to see your fellows succeed, and you want to see the idea come to fruition. There's been a lot of talk about 'ownership', but actually it means a certain determination to see an equal success in the teaching group for each member of staff.

The staff do agree, of course, on the basic values. A measure of difference on points of detail, and the freedom to express it, is regarded as healthy. There has developed at Coombes, therefore, a distinctive culture of collaboration (Nias *et al.*, 1989) with its prominent characteristics of valuing individuals, interdependence, openness and trust (see also Pollard, 1985). Sue spoke of the ability to 'catch messages out of the ether', and being

> deeply aware of the culture that you represent, and constantly enlarging or modifying it, and the way that we beam back to each other what we stand for in very frank discussion. That's probably one of the reasons why our staff meetings meander about a bit, but we're very busy catching clues from each other about what our culture is.

The Coombes staff are a team almost from the point of the interview they have for their job. Carole Davies reported Sue's philosophy as being

'I don't agree with sit-down interviews, you ask me what you want to know.' So I ended up more or less interviewing her. The interviewing process is so often a paper exercise, but she actually gets right down to what people believe education is. The philosophy of Coombes is so important to the way it's run, and that's why it's such a good team, because we all have a similar outlook, and we work well together for the children.

Ray referred to

the whole-team atmosphere, not just between the staff but between the staff and the children and the parents, and everybody that comes in from outside, from the community, visitors from abroad. Everyone's important in making it work.

Even the governors of the school have similar roles. In the legislation of 1988 and afterwards governors were given considerably more power in the new managerial and hierarchical scheme of things. At Coombes, however, they choose to be just as much a part of the community as anybody else. Beryl (governor) explained:

Our meetings are very informal. They're all involved with activities within the school. Our deputy head is very good on the financial side, and we also have an accountant who's a school governor. We have an ex-teacher who's the vice-chairman, so she adds a little bit of professionalism there. And we all work very well together. There's no question of power where we're concerned. The headteacher and her staff are so dedicated to the school that there's no question of the governors wanting to over-rule or exert any power whatsoever. We're behind the staff wholeheartedly.

Team work was part of the general philosophy and applied to all aspects of the educational process. Gina had a 'very shy child' and

at first she was very reluctant to say anything. Now she can't wait to get to school to share something and even if she hasn't got anything she'll try and make something up. She just loves to share her news, or she wants to bring something in to show. She'll come home and say, 'Have you got something brown or blue or red, or Chinese?' and I think that's very important to bring something from home because they want to share it. It all goes in with being part of the family and sharing with other children.

Jenny thought:

The philosophy is the fact that everything is shared together, and the sharing is for everybody and everybody's worth. The child, the adult, and the integration of both is so important and underlines everything that's done in the school.

A supportive community culture

The school has a highly developed sense of partnership and this permeates the work of the school. Parents and the community are drawn into the life of the school by its ethos of valuing all people and this is mutually enriching.

(Ofsted, 1997, para. 23, p. 12)

Parents as co-educators are more often seen as operating in the teacher role in the context of their own homes (Macbeth, 1994). Within school, such a partnership might induce feelings of role ambiguity both among them and among teachers (Thomas, 1989). This is not the case at Coombes, where the very concept of 'role' is not so relevant.

No one's really ever sure who's the teacher, who's the helping mum, who's the teaching assistant, or even who's the head. We've had some funny situations where people have thought that people who are on community service (*by order of the courts*) are actually a member of staff.

(Christine, teaching assistant)

You just wander in and you're met by somebody in wellies who's been mucking out sheep, and you don't know who's who. You don't know who the headteacher is and who the helper is, and it doesn't matter because everybody's important at the school. There's no hierarchy at all, with the children or the teachers. Everybody's got something to say and the children are not in the least bit intimidated by adults. It's not 'Sssh! Be quiet, Teacher's talking'. Everybody's valued.

(Kim, parent)

Liz (teaching assistant) found that 'regardless of what job you do you are treated as an equal'.

The dovetailing of roles applies among the children also:

> If they do have any problems, an older child will look after a younger child, a slower child will attach itself to a quicker child. That child will spend a certain amount of time to give that child enough confidence, and then leave them. They don't go around as buddies, they just mix and match, and that gives them the confidence to talk to various people of various ages in their family groups. They're rubbing shoulders with 5–7-year-olds. So not only are they getting all the wealth of knowledge from the teacher, they're getting all the wealth of knowledge from the group that's around them.

Community service workers are another resource. There is often somebody from the courts serving an order, and on the whole this works well:

> They go and work in the classrooms at times. It's therapeutic for them to be with young children, and it's nice for the children to have another adult model, and somebody younger than the teachers. That's how we get the labour done basically. For instance I've got a couple of really tough lads at the moment. They've put the tables out on the pathways [i.e. for dinner], and they don't mind how much running out to the tables and back they do.

Some work at the school at weekends, under teacher supervision. Sue herself

> might do eight Sundays on the trot, and then I'll work with a whole party of them, perhaps a dozen. We'll start at ten in the morning and finish at four in the afternoon. They'll do some biggish, labouring job that I can't manage, like mixing cement, digging holes, cutting turf, sometimes even playground painting.

These offenders serve orders for minor offences, many being traffic violations. All are carefully vetted by the supervision team. Sue is a strong believer in the idea of community service. She said if she hadn't gone into teaching she would probably have entered the probation service.

We have seen, too, how 'critical others' also played a key role at Coombes, enhancing the charisma of the teacher. Sue overlooked no opportunity to use the knowledge, expertise, experience and equipment of others in advancing her aims. The local shepherd, Hugh, had been coming for nine years to wash and shear the sheep. 'He used to bring a pair of hand shears and do it very slowly, talking to the children while he did it'. Alan, the Traveller, also visited the school. A book records one of his visits, and how he cares for his horse, Jolly Roger. The children helped, using currycombs to groom his coat, cleaning parts of the tackle, observing how Alan cleaned each shoe, and why. The book included excellent black and white photographs, and concluded it was 'A job well done'. This provided an entrée into considering the social and cultural life of travellers, children of whom formed a minority group within the school. Rural craftsmen are invited in to demonstrate their skills – wood-turning, besom-broom-making, carpentry, bread-making, weaving – being part of the school's attempts to trace local traditions. George, the caretaker, exercised his skills in building playground furniture, and contributing to features in the grounds (see Mortimore and Mortimore, 1994, for innovations since 1988 in the role and deployment of associate staff). Hot-air balloonists, helicopter pilots, illustrators (Quentin Blake, Anthony Browne), padres, circus performers, pigeon fanciers, equestrians and many others have demonstrated their skills and shared their experiences at Coombes.

Just as all are teachers, so too all are learners. The knowledge contained and skills imparted in this practice are boundaried and integrated within lives. There are no limits to what might be learned within this framework. Ray noted, 'It's exciting as a teacher and the teachers are really excited to use the grounds as well and we're constantly learning all the time'. Sue Rowe said

> My own science teaching is happening at the same time as the children's. I had poor experiences in my own secondary school and always felt I was a duff on science, and it was only since being here and working here that I've started to develop myself personally. Coombes has given me my grounding. It's seeing me grow daily, it's seen my children very nicely, and everyone who

walks through the doors here, I believe is a beneficiary of it. Everyone is a teacher, the children are teachers as well.

Parents also learn – and teach, like Dee:

> At Ella's last school it was something like 'Oh well, you can come in if you want.' Here, it was 'Well, what can you do? What do you want to come and get involved in?' I come and do a lot of art and painting and model-making with the children, and you just notice how receptive they are to everything that you're doing. They're so enthusiastic about what you can put in, and they've got so many ideas to give back to me that I've learned a lot as well.

Common roles are developed throughout the Coombes community.

> The school has a highly developed sense of partnership and this permeates the work of the school. Parents and the community are drawn into the life of the school by its ethos of valuing all people and this is mutually enriching.
>
> (Ofsted, 1997, para. 23, p. 12)

There is a kind of infectious, cumulative enthusiasm about the place. Sue Humphries rates this the chief ingredient:

> I'd like there to be more people coming in from outside to work and to share their enthusiasms, because it's not always that you need to be talented to come in and work for the children. You really need to be enthusiastic. If you are keen on fossil-collecting, or you're very switched on to the environment and the leaves and the twigs, and what you can do with it in art work, or whatever it is you've got, it's the enthusiasm which is infectious.

The whole community are considered as a learning resource. As we have seen, a large number of people with a wide range of skills visit the school and share their expertise. A school document notes:

> We offer children opportunities to meet, observe, and converse with a wide range of adult models. Every person who crosses

the threshold of the school is valued as a teacher. Our professional role is to provide a laboratory staffed by people with a range of experiences and expertise. Local craftspeople, professionals, parents and visitors work alongside teachers.

There is more than open access. There is involvement. Sue Humphries wanted people to feel that

> they're always going to be welcome, that they come in and watch us teach or, better still, work with us, and that people beyond the community who have talents come in regularly – or even if they don't have any particular talent. It's very much a place where we want the adults to work with the children and to come in and make the atmosphere good for everyone. So it's a sharing place. It's a matter of people seeing a niche for themselves, because there's always room for it here.

The openness is not restricted to the local world. Kim (parent) told us:

> Every culture and race and religion is welcome in this school, and it's accepted that that's the way that country lives, and that's how Chinese or Indian people are. They have a rabbi in to chat to the children, and it's not 'Oh, it's the Jewish religion', it's just a natural process for the school.

A local power base

Coombes may have visionary ideas, but these are of little use without a strong political consciousness. All of the above helps to generate a power base from below. Underwriting this appropriation is a notion of power generated from below around a cause. Kreisberg (1992) has pointed out the limitations of defining power as 'power over', that is a political act of domination, and draws attention to the possibilities of 'power with', that is a strength based on 'relationships of co-operation, mutual support, and equity' (Bloome and Willett, 1991, p. 208). Acting in concert with this is a power deriving from the self. Heath (1993) has written that, while appreciating the influence of external power, 'I believe also that internal motivations and desires to be something special for someone else empower individuals far more than we acknowledge when we talk of what happens within reform efforts of institutions such as schools' (ibid., p. 266).

These two aspects of power – the collective and the individual – interconnect to provide beleaguered schools with chances to promote their aims. Underwriting the Coombes appropriation of the National Curriculum is a theory of power derived from Foucault (1980). For him, power is an ever-present, permeating force in social relations. The 'play' of power in everyday life produces knowledge that goes to the heart of how individuals are constituted. This view of power is positive and productive, rather than repressive and constraining. Two strategical notions from Foucault are relevant to the Coombes analysis. First, the idea of 'surveillance'. He uses the metaphor of the panopticon to make the point of a seat of power with an all-seeing gaze. The analogy is easier to see in relation to a prison where the warders can see all activity from a central point, than a school. In a case like Coombes, however, we might claim that the seat of power is in the school ethos, established, compelling, legitimated, both from which individuals draw to sustain and develop their selves, and to which they contribute, thus consolidating and developing its power.

The Coombes ethos permeates every moment of the day. There is continual reinforcement as one talks to colleagues, prepares lessons, evaluates work, or looks out of a window at children's activity. A common expression used at Coombes is 'That's what it's all about' – a reaffirmation of the ethos through the everyday, and what, to others, might seem trivial behaviour, unworthy of comment. It assails one at every turn. School situations are organised, furnished and decorated to convey the overriding perception of worthwhile knowledge. On one of our visits, the walls displayed photographs and pictures of children planting wild flowers. There was a record of how 'we went on a wild-flower safari'. There were pastel studies of bluebells and daffodils, pictures of sheep and lambs and seed packets pinned on the wall. Seeds were springing up in pots and trays everywhere. Self-made books displayed in the hall included volumes on the uses of pumpkins, on the sun, and the Coombes bog garden, and a wordbook on harvesting. Nature, the earth, and the environment were not the only subjects, but they were pervasive.

The 'surveillance' here operates not through the eyes of a controlling group, as in a prison, but through one's own 'gaze'. Prominent among the messages assailing one's 'gaze' is the discourse through which the ethos is constructed – the second of Foucault's concepts. You see and hear examples of the Coombes discourse every moment of the day, how it is articulated and the purposes it serves. An interesting effect is how the discourse works to transform and subsume other discourses, for example, Coombes recasting the National Curriculum science programme into its own formula.

Coombes's teachers have shown remarkable creativity and energy in incorporating the government's initiatives into the school's organisation and pedagogy while keeping faith with their own beliefs. Coombes could therefore provide a touchstone for the development of a new kind of primary school, one which both takes note of the official policy discourse and reconstructs that discourse in line with their own cherished values.

References

Adams, E. (1990) *Learning through Landscapes: A Report on the Use, Design, Management and Development of School Grounds* (Learning through Landscapes Trust).

Alexander, R. (1992) *Policy and Practice in Education* (London: Routledge).

Alexander, R., Rose, J. and Woodhead, C. (1992) *Curriculum Organisation and Classroom Practice in Primary Schools: A Discussion Paper* (London: HMSO).

Apple, M. (1986) *Teachers and Texts: A Political Economy of Class and Gender Relations in Education* (London: Routledge).

Armstrong, H. E. (1898) 'The Heuristic Method of Teaching; or, the Art of Making Children Discover Things for Themselves: A Chapter in the History of English Schools', reprinted in W. H. Brock (ed.) (1973) *H. E. Armstrong and the Teaching of Science* (Cambridge: Cambridge University Press).

Ashley, M. (1993) 'Tarmacadam Classrooms', *Times Educational Supplement*, 19 March, p. 5.

Atkinson, P. and Delamont, S. (1977) 'Mock-ups and Cock-ups: The Management of Guided Discovery Instruction', in P. Woods and M. Hammersley (eds) *School Experience* (London: Croom Helm).

Ball, S. J. (1981) *Beachside Comprehensive* (Cambridge: Cambridge University Press).

Ball, S. J. (1982) 'Competition and Conflict in the Teaching of English: A Sociological Analysis', *Journal of Curriculum Studies*, 14, 1, pp. 1–28.

Ball, S. J. (1993) 'Education Markets, Choice and Social Class: The Market as a Class Strategy in the UK and the USA', *British Journal of Sociology of Education*, 14, 1, pp. 3–19.

Beetlestone, F. (1998) *Creative Children, Imaginative Teaching* (Buckingham: Open University Press).

Bernstein, B. (1971) 'On the Classification and Framing of Educational Knowledge', in M. F. D. Young (ed.) *Knowledge and Control: New Directions for the Sociology of Education* (London: Collier Macmillan).

Bernstein, B. (1975) *Class, Codes and Control, Vol. 3: Towards a Theory of Educational Transmissions* (London: Hodder and Stoughton).

Blatchford, P. (1989) *Playtime in the Primary School: Problems and Improvements* (Windsor: NFER-Nelson).

Blatchford, P., Creeser, R. and Mooney, A. (1990) 'Playground Games and Playtime: The Children's View', *Educational Research*, 32, 3, pp. 163–74.

Bloome, D. and Willett, J. (1991) 'Towards a Micropolitics of Classroom Interaction', in J. Blase (ed.) *The Politics of Life in Schools* (London: Sage).

Bourdieu, P. and Passeron, J. C. (1977) *Reproduction in Education, Society and Culture* (London: Sage).

Broadfoot, P., Gilly, M., Osborn, M. and Paillet, A. (1993) *Perceptions of Teaching: Primary School Teachers in England and France* (London: Cassell).

Bruner, J. (1986) *Actual Minds, Possible Worlds* (London and Cambridge, MA: Harvard University Press).

Bruner, J. S. (1972) *The Relevance of Education* (Harmondsworth: Penguin).

Bruner, J. S. (1983) *Child's Talk* (Oxford: Oxford University Press).

Bruner, J. S. (1996) *The Culture of Education* (Cambridge, MA: Harvard University Press).

Campbell, R. J. (1993) 'The National Curriculum in Primary Schools: A Dream at Conception, a Nightmare at Delivery', in C. Chitty and B. Simon (eds) *Education Answers Back. Critical Responses to Government Policy* (London: Lawrence and Wishart).

Campbell, R. J., Evans, L., St. J. Neill, S. R. and Packwood, A. (1991) *Workloads, Achievements and Stress: Two Follow-up Studies of Teacher Time in Key Stage 1* (Policy Analysis Unit, University of Warwick).

Cocklin, B., Coombe, K. and Retallick, J. (1996) 'Learning Communities in Education: Directions for Professional Development', British Educational Research Association Conference, 12–15 September, Lancaster.

Coombes (2002) PANDA statistics, Coombes school, Wokingham.

Corrigan, P. (1989) 'In/forming Schooling', in D. Livingstone (ed.) *Critical Pedagogy and Cultural Power* (London: Macmillan).

Craft, A. (2002) *Creativity and Early Years Education* (London: Continuum).

Donaldson, M. (1978) *Children's Minds* (London: Fontana).

Edwards, A. D. and Furlong, V. J. (1978) *The Language of Teaching* (London: Heinemann).

Edwards, D. and Mercer, N. (1987) *Common Knowledge: The Development of Understanding in Classrooms* (London: Methuen).

Egan, K. (1992) *Imagination in Teaching and Learning: Aged 8–15* (London: Routledge).

Fine, G. A. (1994) 'Working the Hyphens: Reinventing the Self and Other in Qualitative Research', in N. Lincoln and Y. Denzin (ed.) *Handbook of Qualitative Research* (London: Sage).

Fisher, R. and Lewis, M. (1999) 'Implementation of the National Literacy Strategy: Indications of Change', ESRC research seminar on raising standards in literacy, May, University of Plymouth.

Foucault, M. (1980) *Power/Knowledge: Selected Interviews and Other Writings* (New York: Pantheon).

Fox, C. (1989) 'Children Thinking through Story', *English in Education*, 23, 2, pp. 33–42.

Fullan, M. and Hargreaves, A. (1992) *Teacher Development and Educational Change* (London: Falmer Press).

Galton, M. and Macbeath, J. (2002) *A Life in Teaching: The Impact of Change on Primary Teachers' Working Lives* (London: National Union of Teachers).

Gitlin, A. D. (1990) 'Education Research, Voice and School Change', *Harvard Educational Review*, 60, 4, pp. 443–666.

Goodson, I. (1983) *School Subjects and Curriculum Change* (London: Croom Helm).

Grugeon, E. (1988) 'Children's Oral Culture: A Transitional Experience', in M. MacLure, T. Phillips and A. Wilkinson (eds) *Oracy Matters* (Milton Keynes: Open University Press).

Grugeon, E. (1993) 'Gender Implications of Children's Playground Culture', in P. Woods and M. Hammersley (eds) *Gender and Ethnicity in Schools: Ethnography Accounts* (London: Routledge).

Hameyer, U. (1996) 'Profiles of Productive Schools', in R. Chawla-Duggan and C. J. Pole (eds) *Reshaping Education in the 1990s: Perspectives on Primary Schooling* (London: Falmer).

Hargreaves, A. (1978) 'Towards a Theory of Classroom Coping Strategies', in L. Barton and R. Meighan (eds) *Sociological Interpretations of Schooling and Classrooms* (Driffield: Nafferton Books).

Hargreaves, A. (1988) 'Teaching Quality: A Sociological Analysis', *Journal of Curriculum Studies*, 20, 3, pp. 211–31.

Hargreaves, D. H. (1991) 'Coherence and Manageability: Reflections on the National Curriculum and Cross-curriculum Provision', *The Curriculum Journal*, 2, 1, pp. 33–41.

Heath, S. B. (1993) 'The Madness of Reading and Writing Ethnography', *Anthropology and Education Quarterly*, 24, 3, pp. 251–68.

Holt, J. (1964) *How Children Fail* (Harmondsworth: Penguin).

Humphries, S. and Rowe, S. (1993a) *The Big Science Book: All about Living* (London: Forbes Publications).

Humphries, S. and Rowe, S. (1993b) *The Big Science Book: Materials and Forces* (London: Forbes Publications).

Hunter, J., Turner, I., Russell, C., Trew, C. and Curry, C. (1993) 'Mathematics and the Real World', *British Educational Research Journal*, 19, 1, pp. 17–26.

Hutchinson, M. M. (1961) *Practical Nature Study in Town Schools* (London: National Froebel Foundation).

Jeffrey, B. (2001) 'Challenging Prescription in Ideology and Practice: The Case of Sunny First School', in J. Collins, K. Insley and J. Soler (eds) *Developing Pedagogy: Researching Practice* (London: Paul Chapman).

Jeffrey, B. (2002) 'Performativity and Primary Teacher Relations', *Journal of Education Policy*, 17, 5, pp. 531–546.

Jeffrey, B. (2003) 'Countering Student Instrumentalism: A Creative Response', *British Educational Research Journal*.

Jeffrey, B. and Woods, P. (1997) 'The Relevance of Creative Teaching: Pupils' Views', in A. Pollard, D. Thiessen and A. Filer (eds) *Children and their Curriculum: The Perspectives of Primary and Elementary Children* (London: Falmer).

Kincheloe, J. L. (1993) *Towards a Critical Politics of Teacher Thinking* (London: Bergin and Garvey).

King, R. A. (1978) *All Things Bright and Beautiful* (Chichester: Wiley).

Kreisberg, S. (1992) *Transforming Power: Domination, Empowerment and Education* (Albany: State University of New York Press).

Lacey, C. (1976) 'Problems of Sociological Fieldwork: A Review of Methodology of 'Hightown Grammar', in M. Hammersley and P. Woods (eds) *The Process of Schooling* (London: Routledge).

Lave, J. and Wenger, E. (1991) *Situated Learning: Legitimate Peripheral Participation* (New York and Cambridge: Cambridge University Press).

Macbeth, A. (1994) 'Involving parents', in A. Pollard and J. Bourne (eds) *Teaching and Learning in the Primary School* (London: Routledge).

Measor, L. (1984) 'Pupil Perceptions of Subject Status', in I. F. Goodson (ed.) *Defining the Curriculum: Histories and Ethnographies of School Subjects* (Lewes: Falmer).

Mortimore, P. and Mortimore, J. (1994) *Managing Associate Staff: Innovation in Primary and Secondary Schools* (London: Paul Chapman).

Moyles, J. (1997) 'Just for Fun? The Child as Active Learner and Meaning Maker', in N. Kitson and R. Merry (eds) *Teaching in the Primary School: A Learning Relationship* (London: Routledge).

NACCCE (1999) *All our Futures: Creativity, Culture and Education* (London: DfEE).

Nias, J. (1989) *Primary Teachers Talking* (London: Routledge).

Nias, J., Southworth, G. and Yeomans, R. (1989) *Staff Relationships in the Primary School: A Study of Organizational Cultures* (London: Cassell).

Ofsted (1997) *Ofsted Inspection of Coombes First School* (London: Ofsted).

Osborn, M., McNess, E. and Broadfoot, P. (2000) *What Teachers Do: Changing Policy and Practice in Primary Education* (London: Continuum).

Pollard, A. (1982) 'A Model of Coping Strategies', *British Journal of Sociology of Education*, 3, 1, pp. 19–37.

Pollard, A. (1985) *The Social World of the Primary School* (London: Holt, Rinehart and Wilson).

Pollard, A. (1992) 'Teachers' Responses to the Reshaping of Primary Education', in M. Arnot and L. Barton (eds) *Voicing Concerns* (London: Triangle Books).

Pollard, A. (1999) 'Towards a New Perspective on Children's Learning', *Education, 3–13*, 27, 3, pp. 56–60.

Pollard, A. and Triggs, P., with, Broadfoot, P., McNess, E. and Osborn, M. (2000) *What Pupils Say: Changing Policy and Practice in Primary Education* (London: Continuum).

Reggio Emilia (1996) *The Hundred Languages of Children* (Reggio Emilia: Reggio Children).

Rowe, S. and Humphries, S. (1994) *Playing around: Activities and Exercises for Social and Co-operative Learning* (London: Forbes Publications).

Rowe, S. and Humphries, S. (2001) 'Creating a Climate for Learning', in A. Craft, B. Jeffrey and M. Leibling (eds) *Creativity in Education* (London: Continuum).

Sarason, S. (1982) *The Culture of the School and the Problem of Change* (Boston: Allyn and Bacon).

Schon, D. A. (1983) *The Reflective Practitioner: How Professionals Think in Action* (London: Temple Smith).

Smith, F., Hardman, F. and Mroz, M. (1999) 'Devaluating the Effectiveness of the National Literacy Strategy: Identifying Indicators of Success', European Conference of Educational Research, 22–25 September, Lahti, Finland.

Smythe, J. (1991) *Teachers as Collaborative Learners* (Buckingham: Open University Press).

Sparkes, A. (1999) 'Exploring Body Narratives', *Sport, Education and Society*, 4, 1, pp. 17–30.

Stebbins, R. (1970) 'The Meaning of Disorderly Behaviour: Teacher Definitions of a Classroom Situation', *Sociology of Education*, 44, 2, pp. 217–36.

Strong, S. (2002) Literacy Conferences Report, *Literacy Today, 31* (London: National Literacy Trust).

Sugrue, S. (1998) *Complexities of Teaching: Child-centred Perspectives* (London: Falmer).

Symes, C. (1992) 'The Aesthetics of Titles and Other Epitextual Devices; or, You Can't Judge a Book by its Cover', *Journal of Aesthetic Education*, 26, 3, pp. 17–26.

Thomas, G. (1989) 'The Teacher and Others in the Classroom', in C. Cullingford (ed.) *The Primary Teacher: The Role of the Educator and the Purpose of Primary Education* (London: Cassell).

Tizzard, B., Blatchford, P., Burke, J., Farquar, C. and Plewis, I. (1988) *Young Children at School in the Inner City* (Lewes: Falmer Press).

Tom, A. (1984) *Teaching as a Moral Craft* (New York: Longman).

Troman, G. and Woods, P. (2001) *Primary Teachers' Stress* (London: RoutledgeFalmer).

Vygotsky, L. (1978) 'The Development of Higher Psychological Processes', in M. Cole, S. Scribner, V. John-Steiner and E. Souderman (eds) *Mind in Society* (Cambridge, MA: Harvard University Press).

Weatley, D. (1992) 'Environmental Education – an Instrument of Change?', in G. Hall (ed.) *Themes and Dimensions of the National Curriculum: Implications for Policy and Practice* (London: Kogan Page).

Westbury, I. (1973) 'Conventional Classrooms, "open" Classrooms and the Technology of Teaching', *Journal of Curriculum Studies*, 5, 2, pp. 91–121.

Woodhead, C. (1995) *Chief Inspector's Annual Report* (London: Ofsted).

Woods, P. (1990) *Teacher Skills and Strategies* (London: Falmer).

Woods, P. (1995) *Creative Teachers in Primary Schools* (Buckingham: Open University Press).

Woods, P. and Jeffrey, B. (1996) *Teachable Moments: The Art of Creative Teaching in Primary Schools* (Buckingham: Open University Press).

Woods, P. and Wenham, P. (1995) 'Politics and Pedagogy: A Case Study in Appropriation', *Journal of Education Policy*, 10, 3, pp. 119–41.

Author index

Subject index